THE ALIEN HUNTER'S HANDBOOK

KINGFISHER
NEW YORK

KINGFISHER
LONDON & NEW YORK

Distributed in the U.S. and Canada by Macmillan, 175 Fifth Ave.,
New York, NY 10010

Colin Jack is represented by Shannon Associates
Geraint Ford is represented by The Art Agency

Developed and edited by Simon Holland
Design and styling by Amy McSimpson

Library of Congress Cataloging-in-Publication data has been applied for.

ISBN: 978-0-7534-6885-2

Kingfisher books are available for special promotions and premiums.
For details contact: Special Markets Department, Macmillan,
175 Fifth Ave., New York, NY 10010.

For more information, please visit www.kingfisherbooks.com

Printed in China
1 3 5 7 9 8 6 4 2
1TR/0712/UTD/WKT/140WF

Note to readers: the website addresses listed in this book are correct at the time
of going to print. However, due to the ever-changing nature of the Internet, website
addresses and content can change. Websites can contain links that are unsuitable
for children. The publisher cannot be held responsible for changes in website
addresses or content, or for information obtained through a third party. We
strongly advise that Internet searches are supervised by an adult.

THE ALIEN HUNTER'S HANDBOOK

HOW TO LOOK FOR EXTRATERRESTRIAL LIFE

Written by
MARK BRAKE

Illustrated by
**COLIN JACK &
GERAINT FORD**

CONTENTS

A PRACTICAL HANDBOOK FOR LIFE HUNTERS

Humans have always gazed up at the stars, but now we are looking more closely than ever. Many of the trillions of stars in space have "planetary systems," which means they have planets and other objects traveling around them. Our Sun (named Sol) is one of these special stars, and its system is known as the solar system. Scientists are looking for other Sun-like stars to see what sort of worlds might be orbiting them. Will any of them be like Earth? Might any of them have life of some kind?

The search for alien life begins right here. On Earth, each part of the planet is different: some areas are freezing cold, some cool, some hot, some very wet, and some very dry. Some parts don't even see much of the Sun. The universe (everything that exists) is like this, too. Other planets have worlds within worlds, with life and landscapes beyond our imagination.

In this book, we will take a step-by-step look at the ways in which we are searching for life in the universe. We will look at what life is and how we might recognize it. We will look at how we can find alien worlds, where life is a possibility. We will consider when it was that alien life could have begun in the universe and what aliens might look like.

We will also think about how we would communicate with extraterrestrials (non-Earth beings). Have aliens already been in contact with Earth and have they visited? Are we ourselves from outer space? Did we arrive in another form, in years gone by, and then develop into what we call "human beings"?

These are all big, big questions, and they will make your brain hurt. So let us begin by being gentle to your brain. Let's consider what makes a living thing a living thing.

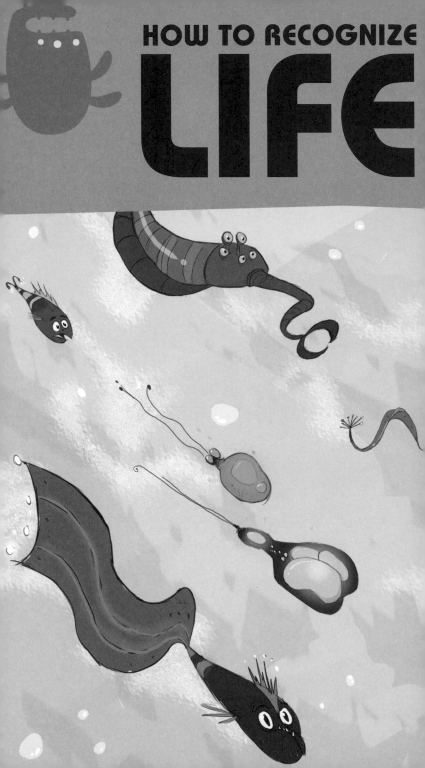

HOW TO RECOGNIZE
LIFE

IT'S ALL ABOUT THE STARS. They fill the universe with their radiant energy. But how and why are they so important to your life and the life of the plants and animals all around you? One thing many living things have in common is that they thrive on energy from stars like the Sun. So read on and bask in this opening chapter, which looks at star stuff, Earthly organisms, and the possibility of life elsewhere in our solar system.

WHAT IS LIFE?

What do we mean by "life"? How can we tell if something is "living"? A home video-game console has a number of parts that all work together, but is it alive? There is a large variety of living things—from microscopic bacteria to trees so big that their tops can't be seen from the ground and from the tiniest insect to the most enormous whale. But no matter how simple or complex, all living things on Earth show the characteristics of life described on these two pages.

LIVING THINGS . . . ARE MADE UP OF CELLS

Living things are organized! Plants and animals are made up of one or more cells. Cells are the building blocks of life. Some organisms, such as bacteria (see page 59), consist of only a single cell (they are "unicellular"). Others, such as humans, are made up of many cells ("multicellular").

LIVING THINGS . . . GROW

Organisms get bigger as they progress from infancy to adulthood. But they grow in an organized way: they increase in size in all of their parts. They don't just gather up stuff willy-nilly. That would be like your arms and legs remaining puny while you grew the biggest of heads!

LIVING THINGS . . . USE ENERGY

All living things get the energy they need from a chemical process called respiration. Animals use respiration to release energy from glucose, the sugar found inside the body's cells. The chemical energy in glucose can be used to provide the energy required for growth, repair, and movement. Plants also use respiration to release energy from food. But, unlike animals, plants are able to make their own food by photosynthesis (see page 14).

LIVING THINGS . . . RESPOND TO THEIR SURROUNDINGS

All organisms respond (react) to things. This can happen in many ways. Tiny bacteria respond to chemicals in their surroundings. When multicellular organisms such as humans respond, it can involve a number of complicated senses. But responses can be simple, too, such as the leaves of a plant turning toward the Sun to receive more light.

LIVING THINGS . . . REPRODUCE

Plants and animals make copies of themselves. They produce offspring (babies). If they make these copies from a single parent, it's called asexual reproduction. If they make copies from two parents, it's known as sexual reproduction. The clever chemical that does the job of copying is called DNA (see pages 59 and 63).

LIVING THINGS . . . EVOLVE

All living things are able to change themselves over a period of time. In other words, they "evolve." This change happens in response to the environment so that they can become better at living in those surroundings. How good a plant or animal is at changing and adapting depends on the organism's DNA, as well as the environment in which it lives.

STAR STUFF!

Stars power our universe. They generate huge amounts of energy, which in turn creates the heat and light that planets (and other bodies) receive. Stars are the building blocks from which the entire cosmos was created. Without our star—the Sun—there would be no light, no life, and no Earth as we know it.

WHAT ARE STARS MADE OF?

All stars are made of gas. Most stars are made of three fourths hydrogen and one fourth helium. Hydrogen and helium are known as "light" elements because their atoms have a very simple structure. But a star's makeup depends on its age. The Sun is a middle-sized star, about five billion years old. More highly evolved stars are made of "heavier" gases. This is because stars "burn" the simpler, lighter elements into heavier ones during the course of their lives.

WHAT HAPPENS INSIDE STARS?

Stars like the Sun burn about 4.4 million tons of gas every second. That's as much energy as seven trillion nuclear explosions every second. The core of a Sun-like star sizzles at more than 18 million°F (10 million°C). This means it is hot enough to fuse (join) hydrogen atoms (extremely tiny particles) together to create a slightly heavier element called helium. This process is known as "nuclear fusion."

WHAT ARE THE "HEAVY" ELEMENTS?

An element is a pure substance made up of only one type of atom. The elements hydrogen and helium make up about 98 percent of all of the ordinary matter (stuff) in the universe—but a tiny two percent of matter is made up of "heavy" elements. These elements have more going on inside them: they have more material in and around the nucleus (the central part) of their atoms.

HOW DO THE ELEMENTS GET SPREAD AROUND?

"Main-sequence" stars, such as the Sun, can keep burning for about ten billion years. Then, as they use up the last of their hydrogen fuel, they begin to swell, pushing their outer layers outward. Eventually, these layers are thrown out into space. This means that the elements created by nuclear fusion are free to be used in the creation of planets and—possibly—life.

Stars are creators
of elements—pure, simple substances that go into the creation of other things.

ARE WE MADE OF STAR STUFF?

Yes. The elements formed inside stars have gone into the makeup of terrestrials (planet-based beings). Hydrogen, carbon, and oxygen are the most important of these elements. They go into the makeup of about 98 percent of all atoms inside the living beings on Earth. These and other atoms were forged inside stars by fusion and then recycled (reused) in space to make new stars, planets, and people.

LIFE GIVER

The Sun is a creator and giver of energy. Almost all organisms on this planet are dependent on this solar energy. Our distance from the Sun is vital. We are 93 million mi. (150 million km) away, which is just the right distance to make our conditions comfortable: any closer would be too hot; any more distant would be too cold.

SOLAR POWER

As the Sun "burns" hydrogen in nuclear fusion, it produces huge amounts of energy. This is how it lights and heats our world, providing a natural source of energy for most of the communities of living organisms on Earth. Any world sitting at the right distance from its local star could potentially receive this kind of life-giving energy.

Sun

GREEN ENERGY

Green plants capture a small part of the solar energy that reaches them. The plants convert the Sun's light energy into food energy, which is then stored inside the plants. This process, known as photosynthesis, uses up carbon dioxide and releases oxygen, which is used in respiration.

Lizard (reptile)

Cricket (insect)

Meat-eating predators (such as the lizard, snake, and eagle) feed on herbivores and sometimes other carnivores, too.

These pink arrows show the flow of energy through the food web.

Vegetation

Herbivores (such as the cricket, rabbit, and field mouse) feed on vegetation.

FOOD WEBS

Energy is passed from one organism to another along a food chain. This happens in an ecosystem (a community of organisms) and usually begins with herbivores, which eat only plants and absorb their energy. The herbivores are then munched by carnivores (meat eaters)—and the carnivores also prey on one another for food energy. In this way, energy is passed around the ecosystem in a tangled circuit called a food web.

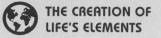 THE CREATION OF LIFE'S ELEMENTS

As you now know, the Sun performs a fiery process called nuclear fusion, in which very simple substances join together to produce new substances, or elements. Elements are the basic building blocks of all matter, including living matter. They go into the creation of all living organisms on our planet.

Eagle (bird)

Rabbit (mammal)

Carbon is an essential part of all living matter on this planet.

CONSTANT CARBON RECYCLING

A lot of nuclear fusion is helped by the element we call carbon. Carbon can act as a catalyst, which means that it speeds up the fusion process but doesn't get used up. This is important! Carbon is formed in stars, and then, much later, it gets recycled as the basis of living organisms (see pages 72–73).

Snake (reptile)

Field mouse (mammal)

15

LIFE EXPLOSION!

Since life began on Earth, it has been evolving in "creeps" and "leaps." For many millions of years, life creeps along with little change happening. But suddenly there are huge leaps. In bursts of feverish activity, enormous changes can occur. Earth is more than four-and-a-half billion years old—so, when we say that these leaps are "sudden," we mean that they happen over millions of years. Compared with billions, millions of years is really quick!

THE CAMBRIAN EXPLOSION

Up until about 580 million years ago, most creatures were quite simple. Then there was a rise in the number of more complex multicellular life forms. This progression led up to the Cambrian period, between 545 and 495 million years ago. During this period, the variety of life began to change to resemble that of today. The body plans of most organisms appeared during the Cambrian explosion, a rapid time of change during the first five to ten million years of the Cambrian period.

THE RISE OF THE BASIC BODY FORMS

In the scientific study of life on Earth, a phylum (plural, phyla) is a group of organisms that all share a similar anatomy (body plan). The best-known animal phyla are: mollusks, sponges, jellyfish, flatworms, roundworms, ringworms, echinoderms, arthropods, and chordates (our group). Although there are 35 animal phyla in total, the nine listed here include more than 96 percent of all animal species on Earth. It was during the Cambrian period that many phyla first appeared. Since then, many species of animal have evolved from the basic body plans that started in this era.

Sanctacaris
had a body made up of many segments and grew to about 4 in. (10cm) long.

Pikaia
was a wormlike creature that swam and fed close to the muddy ocean floor.

Hallucigenia
grew to 1 in. (3cm) at the most but may have been very brightly colored.

Anomalocaris
was a large predator.
Flexible lobes on the sides
of its body helped it push itself
through the water.

CAMBRIAN CREATURES: ANOMALOCARIS

Anomalocaris (meaning abnormal shrimp) was an arthropod. It lived in the oceans of the early to middle Cambrian period. Back then, creatures were small. So, by Cambrian standards, Anomalocaris was a gigantic predator, reaching up to 3 ft. (1m) long. It had a large head, a mouth of 32 overlapping plates, with which it crushed its prey, and two large "arms."

CAMBRIAN CREATURES: OPABINIA

Opabinia was a Cambrian creature that lived on the ocean floor. It was about 1.5–3 in. (4–7cm) long, but was unusual in having five eyes! It had a hollow proboscis, which looked a little like a vacuum cleaner hose. It probably used this tubelike limb to pass food up to its mouth, much like an elephant does today.

Opabinia had five eyes and a special grabbing trunk that brought food to its mouth.

Naraoia
preyed on worms and other small, soft animals on the ocean floor.

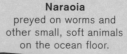

🦎 LIFE HEAVEN . . .

Experts are still trying to define exactly what life is, but the evidence shows that our planet is teeming with it. The more we look, the more we find! Living organisms thrive under the ocean floor, in the polar ice caps—even in orbit, hundreds to thousands of miles above our heads.

Insects once grew to monstrous sizes.

🕷 WHAT MAKES EARTH A PARADISE FOR LIFE?

Water is the key to life. On Earth, water can change from a liquid state into vapor (its gas state) or solid ice and back to water again. This is known as the water cycle. But water can stay in a liquid form across a wide range of temperatures, and Earth is at just the right distance from the Sun to keep water in a liquid state. This allows plant and animal life to thrive.

🕷 A TIME OF GREAT VARIETY

The Carboniferous period took place between about 360 and 300 million years ago. This is when life on Earth really started to vary—more so than during the Cambrian period—with huge tropical rainforests and giant dragonflies, cockroaches, and amphibians, as well as the first examples of reptiles.

The Carboniferous period is named after the carbon-rich coal that formed at that time in Earth's history.

. . . LIFE HELL

Venus is a diabolical planet. It really wouldn't make a great vacation destination. As the weather on a planet is created by its atmosphere (see page 48), it's no wonder the forecast on Venus is so bad. The planet has an atmosphere 90 times thicker than Earth's, plus high winds, blazing heat, and plenty of volcanoes.

It rains acid on Venus, but the rain never reaches the ground!

WHAT MAKES VENUS SO TRICKY FOR LIFE?

Venus suffers from a serious lack of water. You could compare it to the Atacama Desert in Chile, South America. This is one of the driest places on our planet, 50 times drier than the Sahara Desert. Like Venus, the Atacama has no plants, no animals, and no insects in the soil. It's so dry that even bacteria can't survive there.

A TERRIBLE, TERRIBLE ATMOSPHERE

Experts used to think that Venus was Earth's "sister" planet. They believed it might be a giant, swampy world, similar to Earth in its early Carboniferous days (left). But when we sent robotic probes to Venus, they melted in minutes! If you were to visit there, you'd be roasted by the heat and crushed by the immense pressure of its suffocating atmosphere, which is mostly made up of carbon dioxide.

The Russian Venera 9 spacecraft visited Venus in 1975. It released a landing probe—the first one to send back pictures from the surface of another planet.

Many space probes sent to Venus have been melted by the heat and crushed by the pressure of the atmosphere.

DEEP-SEA ALIENS

"Earth" is a strange name for our home planet. About 71 percent of it is covered by ocean, and another one percent by lakes and rivers. So only 28 percent of Earth could be described as "earthy." Life on this planet is thought to have begun in the oceans—and today, water makes up 60–70 percent of all living matter. About 66 percent of the human body is composed of water, and we can live for no more than a week without a drink of it! That's why scientists say that water is the key to life.

LOOKING FOR WATER: THE "MATRIX" OF LIFE

The word "matrix" means an environment or structure in which something, such as a life form, can develop and thrive. The explosive gases of hydrogen and oxygen are the ingredients that make water. They combine to make this most harmless of substances, which is stable (it remains liquid) over a wide range of temperatures. Scientists believe that water could be the matrix of life on other worlds, too. That's why they always "follow the water" when looking for life on other planets.

Deep-ocean vents are often called black smokers. This is because these chimneylike structures belch out superheated water laden with a black cloud of chemicals.

LIFE FORMED IN OUR SEAS

Water plays a vital role in the chemical reactions that create and sustain life on this planet. Because water is necessary for all life—as we know it—to occur, experts think that life probably began in our oceans (about 3,800 million years ago) and then very slowly took hold on land (from about 450 million years ago). So life took a long, long time to emerge from the seas.

DEEP-SEA ECOSYSTEMS

Life may have begun 6,500–10,000 ft. (2,000–3,000m) beneath the surface of the seas in hydrothermal (hot-water) vents. Such vents were first found in 1977. They release water, combined with a cocktail of dissolved minerals, that has been superheated by volcanic activity below the ocean floor. The sea around the vents may be only 36°F (2°C), but the water erupting from the vents ranges from 140° (60°C) to 867°F (464°C)! Undersea explorers have found entire ecosystems there, including fish, giant worms, lobsters, clams, and crabs.

Life around hydrothermal vents does not depend on sunlight for energy. Tiny bacteria get energy directly from chemicals in the water. Larger organisms then feed on the bacteria to get their energy.

Giant tubeworms thrive around these deep-ocean vents.

Squat lobsters are among the many creatures that live and feed around black smokers.

ALIENS ON LAND

On our planet, life now prospers in every nook and cranny. It is flourishing in forests, jungles, rivers, seas, cities, and deserts. All of these habitats are brimming with plants, mammals, birds, insects, reptiles, amphibians, and fish of every known description. But, believe it or not, life on land is a relatively new development.

SIMPLE BEGINNINGS

Life on Earth started roughly 3.8 billion years ago, but it was "basic" for the first 3.25 billion (or so) years. Most creatures were single-celled organisms that lived wherever there was water—in soil, hot springs, around hydrothermal vents, high up in the atmosphere, or deep inside rocks within Earth's crust.

A LEAP OF LIFE: FROM SEA TO LAND!

Tetrapods (four-limbed animals) like us evolved from lobe-finned fish with rounded, fleshy fins that look a little like limbs. These ancestors began to come ashore around 375 million years ago. This is how most large land animals evolved. Some, such as the blue whale, returned to the sea. This major leap of evolution took place during the Devonian Period (around 417–354 million years ago), a long time after the big changes of the Cambrian Period (see page 16).

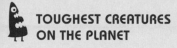

TOUGHEST CREATURES ON THE PLANET

Life can survive in the most extreme environments. Our planet's two icy polar oceans are very inhospitable places, but more than 12,000 living species have been found there. The toughest of them all is a microscopic eight-legged organism known as the water bear, or tardigrade. It can survive temperatures as cold as −459°F (−273°C) and as high as 304°F (151°C). It can stand 1,000 times more radiation than other animals, and it can live without water for up to ten years. In addition to these impressive abilities, it is the only known creature that can survive in the airless vacuum of space.

The water bear,
or tardigrade, is comfortable
in almost any environment.

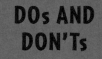

DOs AND DON'Ts

DO: WATCH OUT FOR MICROBEASTS!

Microbeasts ruled our planet for thousands of millions of years. It was only from about 545 million years ago that more complicated creatures arose during a period known as the Cambrian explosion (see pages 16–17). This explosion was the "rapid" appearance, over many millions of years, of most major groups of complex multicellular animals.

DON'T: GO LOOKING FOR HUMANS IN SPACE

So when exploring the Great Unknown, maybe we should look for microbeasts first, not humans. Although there may be millions, or billions, of Earth-like planets in space, the development of life on these worlds might be slower. The path of life may not have begun yet or the life forms may still be at the bacterial, or "microbeast," stage of their development.

LIFE ON MARS

When it comes to life on other planets in our solar system (see pages 30–31), Mars is a planet detective's top suspect. For more than 400 years, we've been spying on its surface through our telescopes. Our studies have revealed that Mars, like Earth, has polar ice caps, seasons, and a 24-hour day. Since the mid-1960s, our robotic spacecraft and surface rovers have sent back a lot of data about the Red Planet. This has helped us learn much more about its mysterious past.

CLUES ON THE SURFACE: EVIDENCE OF ALIENS?

Back in the late 1800s, astronomers thought that marks on the Martian surface were actually canals. They believed that Martians had made these canals to bring water from the polar caps down to the dry areas at the equator (the middle part of the planet). In a way, there is some truth in what they believed: today's experts think that Mars definitely had a warmer and wetter past.

WATER ON MARS: THE LIQUID FACTS

There is only a small amount of water on Mars, locked up in its polar ice caps and soil. But Mars also has its own Grand Canyon, known as the Mariner Valley. Valleys such as these are created by running water wearing away rock over millions of years. So there may have been liquid water sloshing around there at some point in the planet's past. HOW and WHY did Mars lose its surface water?

The canals on Mars
were first observed in 1877
by an Italian astronomer
named Giovanni Schiaparelli.

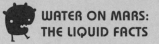

HOW DID MARS LOSE ITS WATER?

Mars has been cold and dry for billions of years. The disappearance of its water could be due to the Martian atmosphere. Mars's atmosphere is so thin that any liquid water on its surface gets quickly evaporated (boiled away) by the Sun's ultraviolet radiation. It is possible, however, that Martian life forms headed under ground as the liquid water on the surface began to evaporate. Below the surface, where the Sun's radiation cannot reach them, regions of liquid water may still exist. Earth has a much thicker atmosphere that holds in surface heat and keeps out most of the Sun's ultraviolet radiation. This prevents our water from evaporating into space.

The Mariner Valley
is named after the Mariner 9 spacecraft that discovered it in 1971–1972. It is three times deeper than Earth's Grand Canyon in Arizona, and would stretch all the way across the United States!

SO . . . WHEN DID THE MARTIANS DIE OUT?!

We've been worrying about Martians ever since they invaded Earth in 1898! In that year, famous novelist H. G. Wells (1866–1946) wrote the first alien invasion story, "The War of the Worlds." Since then, writers and filmmakers have imagined what beings from Mars might look like. But on July 14, 1965, photos taken by the Mariner 4 spacecraft seemed to show that Mars was lifeless.

DOs and DON'Ts

DO: TAKE A LOOK AT MARS THROUGH A TELESCOPE

Bursting with curiosity about stuff on Mars? Amazed that it has polar caps and features that look like Martian-made canals? Then take a good look for yourself. Join an astronomy club!

DON'T: GIVE UP ON THE OTHER PLANETS

It is unlikely there is life on the other planets of our solar system. But we won't really know until we've done a little archaeology on these worlds—in other words, dug them up with a shovel!

LIFE ON MOONS

The idea of life on moons is not new. For hundreds of years, people believed there was life on our Moon. Some thought the craters were actually forts, while others thought they saw winged batpeople through their telescopes! But the more recent exploration of the solar system by robots since the late 1950s has revealed the moons to be real worlds in their own right. Might there be fish swimming in their icy seas, for example?

LIFE COULD EXIST ON MOONS

Each giant gas planet of the solar system (see pages 30–31) has its own group of worlds. They each have a large number of moons orbiting (circling) them. And these moons follow the same "rules of life" as the planets. If the conditions are right, life might evolve on them—even if it is freezing cold out there!

COULD THERE BE LIFE ON EUROPA?

Astronomers believe that Europa, one of the four main moons of Jupiter, may have a deep ocean lying underneath its icy surface crust. Since we believe that life could begin in oceans, Europa might have creatures living around hydrothermal vents (see pages 20–21) deep down in its alien waters.

HOW WOULD LIFE ON EUROPA BEAT THE COLD?

If Jupiter's icy moon Europa does have hydrothermal vents, there could be ecosystems at the bottom of its ocean. On Earth, the sea around a black smoker is about 36°F (2°C). The Europan ocean could be as cold as –328°F (–200°C)—or even colder! But experts believe that Jupiter's gravity (the invisible force of attraction) causes strong tides on Europa, which may make it warmer, allowing life to exist there.

Bioluminescence is a chemical process used by some deep-sea creatures to light up their bodies.

MYSTERIOUS WORLDS

Although Titan is shrouded in a thick, organic haze, scientists have discovered clear evidence of seas on its surface. Enceladus, only one tenth of the size of Titan, probably has an ocean under its surface. The surface has both craters and smooth plains and is covered in water ice.

The true landscape of Titan, once hidden beneath its dense and cloudy atmosphere, was revealed by the Huygens space probe in 2005.

Icy particles shoot up in fountains from the surface of Enceladus. Some of these dazzling specks may now be a part of one of Saturn's rings.

Up to 90 percent of deep-sea life on Earth can use bioluminescence to find food or attract a mate.

EXCITING ENCELADUS

In 2005, the Cassini spacecraft pictured huge ice fountains shooting out of Enceladus, one of Saturn's moons. Because the moon's gravity is weak, these icy particles can soar up to thousands of miles above its surface. Some of them may even be merging with the particles of Saturn's rings! The pull of Saturn's gravity heats the inside of the moon, probably forming an underground ocean of liquid water.

TITAN: IS IT LIKE A YOUNG EARTH?

Titan is the largest moon of Saturn. So far, it is the only moon found to have a dense atmosphere (see pages 48–49). Just like our planet, Titan is a world that is rich in nitrogen. Scientists think Titan has a climate with clouds, wind, and rain. It also has sand dunes, rivers, lakes, and oceans! Although Titan is much colder than Earth, it is rich in the organic ingredients needed to get life going, both on its surface and in its seas.

Ice fish on Earth have chemical features that allow them to survive in very low temperatures. The same could be true of similar creatures on other worlds.

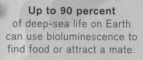

Most of Earth's ocean bottom remains unexplored, so there may still be ocean floor surprises on our home planet.

HOW TO FIND AN ALIEN WORLD

LOCATION, LOCATION, LOCATION! Positioning is important when you move to a new house, but that's nothing when you consider how vital it is to the origins of life itself. In order for an alien world to be capable of hosting life, it needs to be found at a suitable distance from a central parent star. Such stars—and their planetary systems—would also need to be located in the "fertile" regions of galaxies, those vast collections of star- and planet-making materials.

OUR LIFE ZONE

Our solar system is made up of the Sun and all of the bodies traveling in orbit around it. These include rocky inner planets and giant outer planets. The solar system is also home to at least 169 moons, a belt of asteroids, and thousands of smaller bodies such as dwarf planets and comets. All of the objects travel through space together because of gravity, the force of attraction between objects. The Sun is massive, and its strong gravitational pull holds all of the planets in place around it.

SUN	MERCURY	VENUS	EARTH	MARS
	ADS: 36 million mi. (58 million km)	ADS: 67 million mi. (108 million km)	ADS: 93 million mi. (150 million km)	ADS: 142 millic (228 million
	ORBIT: 88 days	ORBIT: 225 days	ORBIT: 365 days	ORBIT: 687
	SIZE: 0.38 x ED	SIZE: 0.95 x ED	SIZE: 1 x ED	SIZE: 0.53 x
	MOONS: 0	MOONS: 0	MOONS: 1	MOONS:

THE HABITABLE ZONE

The habitable zone, or life zone, is the region around a star where orbiting Earth-like planets can thrive and support liquid water. At this distance, carbon-based life may develop (see page 15). Inside this zone, planets and moons are the most likely places where forms of life might be found. The position of a habitable zone inside a planetary system depends hugely on the size and mass of the central star.

SIZE AND SCALE GUIDE

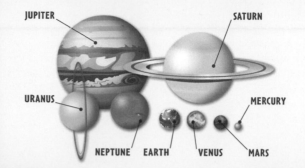

JUPITER
SATURN
URANUS
MERCURY
NEPTUNE   EARTH   VENUS   MARS

JUPITER	SATURN	URANUS	NEPTUNE
ADS: 483 million mi. (778 million km)	ADS: 887 million mi. (1,427 million km)	ADS: 1,784 million mi. (2,871 million km)	ADS: 2,794 million mi (4,497 million km)
ORBIT: 12 years	ORBIT: 29.5 years	ORBIT: 84 years	ORBIT: 165 years
SIZE: 10.93 x ED	SIZE: 9 x ED	SIZE: 3.97 x ED	SIZE: 3.86 x ED
MOONS: 64	MOONS: 62	MOONS: 27	MOONS: 13

WARNING! The Sun and planets are not to scale.

KEY

ADS = average distance from the Sun

ORBIT = length of year: the time it takes to travel around the Sun once, measured in Earth days or years

SIZE = diameter (thickness) compared with Earth's diameter (ED)

STARS AND PLANETS: HOW ARE THEY DIFFERENT?

The Sun and Jupiter both contain lots of hydrogen and a smaller amount of helium, and yet they are very different. The Sun is a star and Jupiter is a planet. Their main difference is that the Sun is more massive and therefore hot enough inside to burn its hydrogen gas. Jupiter is not massive enough for this to happen. But for planets much more massive than Jupiter, which includes some Hot Jupiters (see page 42), the boundaries begin to get blurred. Experts have come up with the idea of a "planemo." A planemo is a body with a huge mass that can still be called a planet but that does not have enough mass to become a star.

GOLDILOCKS ZONES

In a planetary system such as ours, scientists think a planet must lie inside the habitable zone to support life. If a planet is beyond the outer limits of the life zone, it will not get enough of its sun's energy and water (if it has any) will freeze. If a planet is within the life zone's inner limits, it will get too much solar energy and any surface water will boil away. The habitable zone is neither too hot nor too cold, which is why some experts refer to the habitable zone as the "Goldilocks" zone.

OTHER SOLAR SYSTEMS ARE OUT THERE!

For centuries, astronomers have wanted to know how many stars in space have planets orbiting them. Details from NASA's Kepler mission (see page 36) have convinced today's astronomers that there are at least 50 billion planets inside our own galaxy (see pages 34–35). They also think that more than half of all of the Sun-like stars in the Milky Way are "parent" stars, which means that they do have planets and moons around them.

THE HOT ZONE: LIFE IN THE BOILER

Planets in the hot zone are close to their parent star. They become "locked" to the star so that the same side of the planet always faces its star. (The Moon faces us in a similar way. We cannot see its far side from Earth.) These planets have high-speed winds that transfer heat from the sunlit side across to the dark side. So even though only one half receives sunlight, the average temperature of the two sides is actually quite similar.

In the hot zone, temperatures are far too high for life to exist.

In the cold zone, water is locked up as solid ice.

In the life zone, the temperature range is just right for liquid water—and life.

THE HABITABLE ZONE: "JUST RIGHT" FOR LIFE!

A habitable planet sits in the life zone, the Goldilocks zone. The name comes from the story of "Goldilocks and the Three Bears", in which the little girl chooses Baby Bear's porridge, because it is neither too hot nor too cold, but "just right." The temperature range of a Goldilocks planet is also "just right," so that liquid water can stay on its surface.

THE COLD ZONE: WORLDS OF MYSTERY

The cold zone begins at the "frost line." This imaginary line marks the distance from the star where it is cold enough for hydrogen compounds (such as water, methane, and ammonia) to be frozen solid. The average temperature for this is about −189°F (−123°C). The frost line in our own solar system lies around the middle of the asteroid belt, between Mars and Jupiter.

GALACTIC LIFE ZONES

To support life, a planet needs to be in the life zone around its parent sun. But that's not all. Scientists think that a planet ALSO has to be in the right part of its galaxy. Galaxies are the vast system of stars in which most suns live. Just like planetary systems in orbit around stars, galaxies also have habitable zones where the conditions will be more favorable for the development of living things.

GALAXY LOCATION

A habitable planetary system must be in the right part of a galaxy. It cannot be too close to the center, because of the high levels of harmful radiation there. But it cannot be too far from the center either. The galactic center is where a lot of the heavy elements are found. For this reason, the area surrounding the center is thought to be a fertile region for rocky planets (see page 35).

Our galaxy, known as the Milky Way, is a barred spiral galaxy.

THE LIFE ZONE INSIDE A GALAXY

In our galaxy, the life zone (colored green, above) contains about six billion stars. It is roughly 6,000 light-years wide, and its outer limit stretches to around 25,000 light-years from the galaxy's core (central region). Other galaxies have larger or smaller life zones, depending on their characteristics and the materials they contain.

SOLAR SYSTEM KEY

▬▬▬	Orbit of MERCURY
▬▬▬	Orbit of VENUS
▬▬	Orbit of EARTH
▬▬▬	Orbit of MARS
⌇⌇⌇⌇	Orbit of ASTEROID BELT
▬▬▬	Orbit of JUPITER

YOU ARE HERE!

Our Sun, along with planet Earth and the rest of the solar system, orbits the center of the Milky Way galaxy. It takes the Sun around 250 million years to orbit this giant galactic center. This is known as a cosmic year.

Our solar system orbits the center of the Milky Way.

SUN

SUN

☾ THE IMPORTANCE OF THE HEAVY ELEMENTS

In space, a heavy element is any pure substance that is more complex than the simplest elements, hydrogen and helium. Heavy elements are important materials in the formation of rocky planets. Earth is mostly composed of heavy elements such as oxygen, silicon, nickel, and iron. Scientists think that these elements are also needed to create complex life.

LENTICULAR GALAXY

RING GALAXY

GALAXY TYPES

BARRED SPIRAL GALAXY

ELLIPTICAL GALAXY

There are billions of galaxies in the universe. A few common types are shown here. Most galaxies fall into three main categories that describe how they look: spiral, elliptical (egg shaped), and irregular (with no specific shape). Spiral galaxies are sometimes "barred," with a central bar-shaped structure made up of stars.

EXOPLANETS

An exoplanet (short for "extrasolar planet") is any planet outside our solar system. We have discovered hundreds of these weird and wonderful worlds and continue to look for hundreds more. Great planet-finding missions are already in progress. The focus is on locating rocky planets like Earth where we may be more likely to find life.

ROCKY AND GASSY PLANETS

In our solar system, there are two types of planets: rocky and gassy. The rocky ones formed much closer to the Sun in the warm or hot zones. The gassy ones formed farther out, beyond the frost line, a long way into the cold zone. These outer planets (known as the "gas giants") are mostly composed of gas, but the gas is under so much pressure that it becomes liquid in the planets' deeper layers. We believe that they each have a rocky core.

THE KEPLER MISSION: A SEARCH FOR EARTHS

The most exciting quest for exoplanets so far is NASA's Kepler mission. Kepler is a space observatory that looks for Earth-like planets orbiting middle-sized stars like the Sun. Kepler scans the sky, looking for mini eclipses—the telltale signs of an exoplanet crossing in front of its parent star (see pages 38–39). The aim of the Kepler mission is to find out how many of the billions of stars in our galaxy have Earth-like planets.

Rocky planets have solid surfaces so that you can land your spaceship!

TIMELINE OF EXOPLANET DISCOVERY

2008: a message is beamed from Earth to the Gliese 581 star system, which may have Earth-like planets.

2002: the 100th exoplanet is discovered.

1995: 51 Pegasi b discovered—the first exoplanet to be found around a Sun-like star.

February 17, 1600: Giordano Bruno is burned at the stake for heresy (going against the beliefs of the Church).

1584: Italian friar and astronomer Giordano Bruno says there are "countless suns and countless Earths all rotating around their suns."

Gassy planets
would crush and swallow
your spaceship!

The Kepler space observatory
has already begun to find Earth-sized
planets (see page 104).

HISTORY'S
PLANET PIONEERS

2029:
the message
beamed from
Earth is due to reach
the Gliese 581 system.

November 2011: the U.S.
government announces
it has no evidence that life
exists outside our planet.

November 21, 2011: the
700th exoplanet is
discovered.

February 2011: NASA says
that the Kepler Mission has
discovered 1,235 unconfirmed
planets orbiting around
997 parent stars.

March 6, 2009: the
launch of NASA's
Kepler space
observatory.

Ancient Greek philosopher
Democritus was one of the first people to
believe that the universe contained many
worlds like Earth. Seventeenth-century
German mathematician Johannes Kepler
is the man after whom NASA's Kepler
mission is named. One of the greatest
astronomers of all time, Kepler dreamed
of space travel and wrote one of the
first-ever science-fiction stories,
about aliens living on the Moon.

Democritus
(c. 460 B.C.–c. 370 B.C.)

Johannes Kepler
(1571–1630)

37

WOBBLY STARS

Compared with the stars they travel around, exoplanets are very faint points of light. They are usually about one million times fainter than their parent star (or stars). Trying to find them is like looking for a needle in a haystack: among the first 700 exoplanets to be found, only about ten of them were "seen" by images created using telescopes. In order to locate the rest, scientists have had to use other ingenious methods of detection.

ECLIPSES OF LIGHT

In space, an eclipse happens when one body passes into the shadow of another. An eclipse of the Sun happens when it moves into the shadow of the Moon so that the Sun cannot be seen from Earth. If an exoplanet crosses in front of its parent star, it may cause a mini eclipse. This gives astronomers a chance to locate the planet. This detection method is known as transit photometry.

SEARCHING FOR WOBBLY STARS

There are three main ways of locating exoplanets. So far, astronomers have found most of them by looking for tiny changes in the spectrum of light emitted by a parent star. The oldest method is known as "astrometry": this is when a star "wobbles" as it travels through space. This wobble may be caused by the gravitational pull of a planet (or planets) around it, tugging on the star. By measuring the size of the wobbles, experts can guess how big the tugging planets are. For the third method, see "Eclipses of Light" (below).

OUR WOBBLY SUN: THE "JUPITER EFFECT"

Imagine alien astronomers out there in space. If they studied our solar system, they would see a wobbly Sun! Like all stars with planets, our Sun wobbles. The combined gravity of the planets is what causes the Sun to quiver. Mighty Jupiter is bigger than the other planets put together, so it exerts the most massive tug of all.

WHAT THE PLANET HUNTERS FIND

So far, looking for wobbly stars is the best way of finding exoplanets. Hundreds of them have been discovered in this way. Planet hunters look for twitchy stars out to about 160 light-years from Earth. The "Jupiter effect" means that they may find a very large planet in orbit around a wobbling star. Because bigger, more massive planets create bigger wobbles, this method of planet hunting is perfect for finding other giant Jupiter-like worlds. But it's not so good for finding other Earth-like worlds.

A SOLAR ECLIPSE
The Moon passes between the Sun and Earth.

A MINI ECLIPSE
An exoplanet can be found as it moves in front of its parent star.

EX⊙PLANET ZO⊙

The discovery of exoplanets is an exciting science. Dreaming up fictional planets has long been a hobby of science-fiction writers, but now the universe has them beaten. It has conjured up the possibility of planets that it would be difficult for anyone to imagine. You could say there's a "zoo" of exoplanets out there!

Life on a diamond planet
is unlikely . . . but wouldn't a carbon fungus be fun?!

TWINKLE, TWINKLE! WORLDS OF CARBON

Diamond is a colorless crystalline form of pure carbon, and some planets out in space may be composed of this material. Such carbon-rich worlds may be found in orbit around pulsars, stars that are the leftovers of a supernova (the explosive death of a massive star). Despite their small size, these worlds would have more mass than Jupiter, and a very high density (compactness). Experts believe that supernova explosions leave behind a lot of this crystalline carbon, which could then form planets.

GAS WORLDS

Gas worlds are thought to be common. They're often massive planets that have a thick atmosphere of hydrogen and helium, like Saturn's and Jupiter's. Or they might have a thin outer covering of gas—as the "ice giants" Uranus and Neptune do. Many have a dense rocky core (center).

TILTED GLOBES

Earth rotates on a slightly tilted axis as it orbits the Sun. Some rocky planets could be tipped over onto their sides, perhaps owing to a collision with a massive object. The tilt creates curious climates and seasons, with the north and south poles getting more sunlight than the equator!

DIAMOND PLANET

GAS WORLD

"HEAVILY TILTED" EARTH-LIKE PLANET

GO FISH!
WORLDS OF WATER

An ocean planet, or water world, is a planet where the surface is completely covered by liquid water. The icy worlds of the outer solar system are roughly half frozen water, half rock. If icy exoplanets in other systems were to drift closer to their sun, their ice would melt in this warmer orbit, creating ocean worlds fit for life. Their oceans would be hundreds of miles deep, with huge waves running across the surface of their vast seas.

Ocean planets could be home to all sorts of aquatic creatures.

Firebirds are the stuff of fiction. But who knows what might exist on such a world!

HOT STUFF!
WORLDS OF FLAME

The idea of a planet plagued with flames is surely horrendous. But such a world is easily imagined. A rocky planet orbiting too close to its sun would not just be boiling hot. The star's gravity would torment the little world, resulting in extreme forces that would bend and buckle the planet's surface. Such a tortured world would be inhospitable to life, violently volcanic, and covered in oceans of bubbly lava.

CANNONBALL WORLDS

Earth has a core of molten iron covered in a crust of rock. Some planets could have iron cores and a crust that's been almost completely blasted off by a huge impact. This would leave a strange world, almost entirely made of iron. Even so, it still might have oceans and an atmosphere.

RED DWARF PLANETS

Red dwarf stars are the most common types of stars. They have less mass than our Sun and are cooler, so their Goldilocks zones are closer to them. They also have extremely long life spans, which would give life plenty of time to evolve on any planets orbiting in their habitable zones.

FIRE PLANET

CANNONBALL WORLD

OCEAN PLANET

RED DWARF PLANET

HOT JUPITER!

Hot Jupiter planets, or "roaster planets," are a common type of exoplanet. They are named after Jupiter because their mass is as great—or greater—than that of Jupiter, the largest planet in our own solar system. Hot Jupiters orbit their own stars at a much closer distance than Jupiter orbits our Sun. So far, most of the exoplanets we have discovered are more massive than Jupiter, but astronomers are confident that a wider variety of exoplanets will be located as time goes by.

Hot Jupiter planets move closer to their parent star once they are fully formed.

The very strong gravity of Hot Jupiter planets causes their parent star to "wobble," making them easier to detect.

WHY ARE THERE SO MANY JUPITERS ...

Hot Jupiters are the easiest exoplanets to discover when using the "wobbly stars" method (see pages 38–39). Because they are so massive, they cause a large and rapid trembling in their parent star, making their presence simpler to detect. When detection methods improve, experts expect to find many smaller planets, perhaps similar in nature to our own.

... AND WHY ARE THEY SO 'HOT'?

Because they're so close to their parent star! Astronomers have discovered that Hot Jupiter planets lie between ten and 300 times closer to their central star than Jupiter is to our Sun. Naturally, this makes them sweltering hot. In fact, their gassy atmospheres get completely stripped away by the intense heat.

51 PEGASI B

Perhaps the most famous Hot Jupiter is 51 Pegasi b. If you don't want to use its official title, its nickname is Bellerophon. This exoplanet was discovered in 1995 by Swiss astrophysicist Dr. Michel Mayor and his student Didier Queloz. It was the first exoplanet ever to be detected around a Sun-like star (or main-sequence star). 51 Pegasi b is so famous that all other Hot Jupiters are sometimes referred to as "pegasids," or pegasean planets, in honor of this great discovery.

Sun-like stars such as this one are always being looked for by planet hunters.

51 Pegasi b   51 Pegasi (Sun-like star)

51 Pegasi b is so close to its parent star that it races around it in only 4.2 Earth days. The years on this planet fly by!

DO HOT JUPITERS STAY IN THE SAME PLACE?

Hot Jupiters are all thought to have started life at a much greater distance from their parent star. Scientists believe that they are initially created beyond the frost line (see page 33), where the planets can form from rock, ice, and gases. Then they appear to migrate inward toward their sun, taking up their present red-hot positions at "star central."

43

THE BIG PRIZE

For planet hunters around the globe, the ultimate goal—the prize of all prizes—is to find a super-Earth. Super-Earths are exoplanets that are more massive than Earth but much smaller than gas giants such as Jupiter. The word "super" in their name refers to how big they are. It does not mean they are superplanets with a supertemperature or superpowers! Some scientists use the term "gas dwarf" instead of super-Earth, but that is not quite as fun.

Super-Earths
are a big catch for planet hunters all around the world. In size, they may be between two and ten times the mass of planet Earth.

THE ULTIMATE PRIZE: ANOTHER EARTH

Over the last 500 years or so, writers and scholars have imagined life in space—and often they have dreamed of a planet just like Earth. When we think about life elsewhere, we often compare it to life on Earth, which is based on water and carbon (see pages 72–73). We often consider a super-Earth to be the best of all discoveries because, rightly or wrongly, we expect the conditions on this type of exoplanet to produce Earth-like life.

The Kepler 22 b planet was first spotted in 2009, and in December 2011, astronomers confirmed its position inside a Goldilocks zone.

HOW TO FIND SUPER-EARTHS

Finding a super-Earth is just like finding any other type of exoplanet. Scientists look for star "wobbles" and mini eclipses (see pages 38–39) using data from both ground- and space-based telescopes. The Kepler space observatory is on the lookout for Earth-like planets. It has already located a super-Earth, named Kepler 22 b, that is orbiting a Sun-like star within the star's habitable zone.

ARE SUPER-EARTHS EASY TO FIND?

When planet hunters speak about super-Earths, they are usually talking about exoplanets that are less than ten times Earth's mass. So far, they don't completely agree on how small a super-Earth can be. Some say two Earth masses and some say five. But because super-Earths are bigger than Earth-sized planets, they will be easier to detect, as they will make a bigger "quiver" in their parent star.

Traveling to a super-Earth could take hundreds or even thousands of years.

GLIESE 581 G

Gliese 581 g is the fourth planet away from a red dwarf star named Gliese 581. Planet hunters believe that the planet sits in the habitable zone of its system and that it is a rocky planet fit for liquid water. So it may also be suitable for life. It is about three to four times the mass of Earth, so it is classed as a super-Earth.

HOW TO NAME AN EXOPLANET

An exoplanet's name depends on the name of the parent star and its position around it. The second planet in orbit around the star Tau Boötis A is named Tau Boötis A b. The scientific name for our Sun is "Sol," and Earth is the third planet away from it. So our planet's formal exoplanet name would be Sol c. Gliese 581 g should really be Gliese 581 d, but it was found after its fellow planets had already been named.

EXOTIC WORLDS

There are enough planets orbiting other stars to give every person who has ever lived on Earth, back to our prehistoric ancestors, their very own private world-sized home. But how many of those places are inhabited and by what kinds of life? Such worlds may be a million times farther away than Mars, but one day we might explore them. What would we find?

PLANETS AROUND A RED DWARF

Red dwarf stars are small and cool: they have less than one half of the mass of the Sun. Experts once thought that red dwarfs were unable to support habitable planets, but now they think otherwise. They DO have planets, but the planets have strange orbits. A planet around a red dwarf always shows the same face to the star. It is "locked" by gravity, with one half always in darkness and the other side always bathed in sunlight.

LIFE IN THE TWILIGHT ZONE

Red dwarf worlds are weird and exotic. On their dark side is a vast and frozen wasteland. On their light side are oceans, land, and mild weather conditions. But there is also a "twilight zone" between the light and dark halves. In these dimly lit regions, strange creatures may compete for food and light.

Birdlike predators (right) may prey on slow-moving amphibians in the twilight zone. They might be swift, traveling at more than 37 mph (60km/h).

Amphibian-like beasts (left) would prefer the wetter, muddier parts of the twilight zone.

"Sky whales" might be up to ten times heavier than anything that has ever flown on Earth.

"Balloon" plants might have a bulblike bladder filled with hydrogen gas, produced by bacteria inside them.

Tethers could control their height, allowing the bladder to rise and fall in order to collect sunlight for photosynthesis.

MOONS OF GAS GIANTS

Gassy exoplanets are unlikely to harbor life, but their moons might. Imagine an Earth-sized moon orbiting a massive gas giant. This moon is a rocky world of oceans and continents, with an atmosphere that is much richer in oxygen and carbon dioxide than Earth's. Plants need carbon dioxide to make their food during photosynthesis (see page 14), so plant life is far more abundant here than on Earth.

LIFE ON AN EARTH-SIZED MOON

Life on such a world could be mind-blowing. Scientists have imagined sky whales, giant flying creatures that can scoop up small airborne plants and animals with their huge mouths. They might weigh the same as a small killer whale, with a wingspan of up to 30 ft. (10m). Balloon plants may also exist here, with huge gas-filled bladders that float high up into the atmosphere.

47

AIRLESS WORLDS

Air is another name for Earth's atmosphere, the thin blanket of gases that surrounds our planet. Most planets—and some moons—in the solar system have atmospheres, but they are very different from our own. Some planets have one that is made up of toxic chemicals, while other big planets are "all atmosphere" and no solid surface. Earth is the only planet we know of that has an atmosphere that makes life possible.

EARTH'S ATMOSPHERE: A LIFE-SUPPORT SYSTEM

Our atmosphere is made up of about 78 percent nitrogen, 21 percent oxygen, 0.9 percent argon, 0.04 percent carbon dioxide, and the rest is water vapor and tiny amounts of other gases. It provides oxygen for all living things to breathe and makes it possible for liquid water to exist on Earth's surface. It also shields us from almost all harmful types of radiation from the Sun, steadies the planet's temperature, and protects us from most meteoroid impacts.

"LEAKY" WORLDS

The thickness of an atmosphere depends on two things: gravity and temperature. A world with weaker gravity may not be able to hold onto the gas molecules in its atmosphere. Gas molecules also move faster when they are warmer, so a cooler atmosphere is much better at preventing the molecules from escaping into space.

The force of gravity, which attracts objects toward one another, is what holds an atmosphere in place.

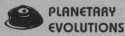

PLANETARY EVOLUTIONS

In our solar system, all of the planets started out with atmospheres of hydrogen and helium. The four inner planets (see page 30) then lost these atmospheres. Over time, they gained a "secondary atmosphere" made up of gases released from their own insides—from volcanoes, for example. Mercury and Mars, however, have lost their secondary atmospheres as well.

Without portable life-support systems, human travelers would not be able to breathe the "air" on planets such as Venus and Mars, where the atmosphere is 95 percent carbon dioxide.

THE PLANETARY GREENHOUSE EFFECT

The early days on Venus were probably similar to those on Earth. Around four billion years ago, Venus may even have had liquid water on its surface. But the rising levels of gases such as carbon dioxide in Venus's atmosphere led to a "greenhouse effect." This has trapped the heat from the Sun, resulting in sizzling temperatures and the loss of all water.

THE RISE OF OXYGEN LEVELS ON EARTH

The sharp rise of oxygen in Earth's atmosphere is due to the appearance of a simple form of bacteria about 2.5 billion years ago (see page 59). This bacteria lived on the energy from the Sun and carbon dioxide in the oceans, giving out oxygen as a waste product.

Sound cannot travel in a vacuum (airless environment), so headphones would be needed for a party on a world with no atmosphere.

ODD ORBITS

The universe is full of patterns, but there's plenty of room for things that don't quite fit in. With so many possibilities in so many different places, small oddities often pop up. Maybe a planet's orbit around a star is just too irregular for its own good. Maybe a star has become lost and confused, roaming around the cosmos. There are also "rogue" worlds, that sit between galaxies (star systems).

Charon is the largest of about four known moons around Pluto.

Pluto is no longer considered to be a planet . . . But it is still the tenth most massive object orbiting the Sun.

PLUTO'S PUZZLING PATH

We used to call Pluto a planet. However, it has a highly tilted and elliptical (oval-shaped) orbit that overlaps with the orbit of Neptune. In order to count as a planet, it needs to have cleared its orbit of all other objects. This is one reason why it was reclassified as a dwarf planet in 2006. Its new name is 134340 Pluto.

PLUTO'S ORBIT

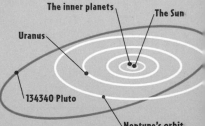

The inner planets

The Sun

Uranus

134340 Pluto

Neptune's orbit

Planet X hides behind its map of the outer solar system. Is it lost or just hiding?

The Sun is, on average, about 3.7 billion mi. (6 billion km) away from Pluto.

LOST PLANET: PLANET X

After Neptune was found in 1846, astronomers began looking for more distant planets. They noted the strangeness of Neptune's orbit and thought the gravity of a further planet might be to blame. So the search for "Planet X" began. Even though Pluto was found in 1930, some experts think Planet X may still be out there somewhere, hiding in the dark.

FREE-FLOATING PLANETS

Pluto is not the only oddball. Rogue planets, or orphan planets, have been thrown out of their planetary systems, and are no longer tied to the gravity of a parent star. Instead, they follow a different orbit around their home galaxy. Some scientists believe there may be twice as many Jupiter-sized rogue planets as there are stars.

STAR OUTCASTS

Stars can also be a little wayward. Intergalactic stars do not belong to a galaxy but exist in intergalactic space (the space between galaxies). This may occur if two immense galaxies collide, tossing the stars out into the huge, yawning void. One trillion intergalactic stars are thought to exist in the Virgo Cluster (a vast group of galaxies) alone.

Some rogue planets wander in darkness, orbiting a galaxy instead of a star.

TIME HAS BEEN TICKING AWAY FOR BILLIONS OF YEARS. Roughly 13.75 billion years, as a matter of fact. That is the overall approximate age of the universe. It's an ancient place! In this chapter, we will look back through time and consider how long life beyond Earth has had to begin and develop. We will ask: if a race of aliens began and evolved during the early stages of the universe, how smart might they be?

COSMIC TIME.

Until about 300 years ago, scientists thought that the entire "history of everything" was only about 6,000 years old. But the discovery of fossils (the remains of living things preserved in stone) and the study of rocks and their ages has shown that time is much more ancient! Planet Earth is roughly 4.5 billion years old, and the universe has been around for about 13.75 billion years. So, seeing as life has had ALL of that time to develop, when might alien life have started?

The building blocks of life did not appear at the moment of the big bang. They formed from simple elements over a very, very long period of time.

The simple elements of hydrogen and helium were created in the big bang. They make up 98 percent of the universe.

BEHOLD! THE DAWN OF TIME

Scientists believe that the universe started with the "big bang." Their theory states that space and time began with an explosion of dense matter around 13.75 billion years ago. The early universe was hot, but eventually it cooled down to form atoms. These atoms formed the light elements of hydrogen and helium. The heavier elements were created later, inside stars.

Metals are made inside stars and supernovae (the explosions of massive stars) and are a crucial component in rocky planets such as Earth.

Carbon is formed inside stars and gets recycled. It is the basis of all known life.

Oxygen is also made by stars. It is a key ingredient in life's most vital liquid—water.

ALIENS NEED PLANETS

Where might aliens live and when? If it is true that water (or some other liquid) will always be the matrix of life (see page 20), aliens will be able to evolve only on rocky planets with a solid surface and an atmosphere that allows liquids to remain on the surface (see page 48). Planets form from the dusty disks of material that surround young stars. Scientists disagree about how long it took the universe to develop before enough materials were available for rocky planets such as Earth to form (see below).

LIQUID CLUES

Where there's liquid, there may be life. Mars had a warm and watery past. There may be fishy seas under the icy crust of Europa, one of Jupiter's four main moons. Huge lakes of liquid methane exist on Titan, Saturn's largest moon. This all points to the possibility of life's existence in these places, either in the past or in the future. The same may be true of other worlds beyond our solar system.

ARE ALIEN RACES YOUNG OR OLD?

The first stars formed from nothing but hydrogen and helium. Today, now that the universe is well developed, stars are able to form from collapsing clouds of gas and dust, which contain more planet-building ingredients. So some experts think that it was impossible for Earth-like planets to form in the early universe. But if they had done so, there might already be many ancient alien civilizations around, all highly evolved and very smart.

SOLAR SYSTEM EVOLUTION

How do stars and planets behave in deep space? How are they made and how do they evolve? The better we know our solar system, the better we can answer these questions. Planets and stars in other systems may follow similar patterns to those of our Sun and its family of planets and moons.

4,750 MYA: leftovers of a supernova explosion contain gassy and dusty materials.

4,650–4,500 MYA: a HUGE cloud of gas, the remains of the supernova, collapses to form the young Sun and planets.

4,500 MYA: Earth survives a collision with another young planet. Our Moon forms around the Earth out of the bits and pieces created by the collision.

1) WHICH MATERIALS FORMED THE SOLAR SYSTEM?

Our solar system formed as the result of a shock wave from an exploding star (a supernova). This triggered the collapse of a dense, dusty cloud of material. Most of the material gathered in the center, forming the Sun, while the rest of it flattened into a swirling disk that formed the planets, moons, and other planetary bodies.

2) HOW DID WE END UP WITH THE MOON?

There are many theories about the formation of the Moon, but here is the one that most experts believe: the "big splash" theory says that a planet-sized body, roughly the same size as Mars, hit young Earth and sent lots of "moonlets" into orbit around our planet. Eventually, they all came together to form the Moon.

6) WHY ARE THE OUTER PLANETS GASSY?

Farther away from the infant Sun, the temperatures were much cooler. These frosty conditions enabled the lightweight gases (in the disk of material) to condense into icy particles that then began to clump together. The outer planetesimals continued to grow in this way until they became gassy giants.

5) WHY ARE THE INNER PLANETS ROCKY?

Close to the young Sun, the temperatures were very high. This caused lightweight elements, such as hydrogen and helium, to evaporate (turn to vapor). But the temperature was ideal for the heavier rocky and metallic elements to condense into particles that then clumped together into rocky planetesimals.

4,100 MYA: the surface of Earth cools down enough for the rocky crust to solidify.

4,500–4,450 MYA: the core of the Sun becomes hot enough to burn hydrogen gas. It becomes a star.

3) HOW AND WHEN DID THE SUN START BURNING?

Around 50 million years after the birth of the solar system, the core of the Sun became hot enough to burn hydrogen gas. A star was born! All stars burn hydrogen as their main fuel, converting it into helium as they do so (see page 12). The Sun will continue doing this for roughly another five billion years to come.

4) HOW DID THE PLANETARY BODIES FORM?

As the Sun evolved, the planets took shape out of the swirling disk. Experts think that grains of gas and dust clumped together to make "planetary embryos." Small at first, at only 650 ft. (200m) wide, these clumps soon made tiny planets called planetesimals. They gradually merged together, too, and grew to form the young planets.

TIME FOR LIFE

So you know how old cosmic time is and how stars and planets evolve. But when does a planet or moon enter its "time for life"? When are planetary conditions ripe for the beginning and evolution of aliens? To give you an idea, here is a timeline showing how life on Earth got started.

1) BOMBARDMENTS: THE SNUFFING OUT OF LIFE

Getting walloped by a large object is what planets had to put up with in the early solar system. So if any life developed early on, it was in danger of being wiped out by the high rate of impacts—though some single-celled organisms may have survived in deep ocean vents (see pages 20–21).

2) EARTH DEVELOPS AN OCEAN

Earth's oceans had various sources. Some water was already there in the materials that made the planet. The "big splash" that made the Moon may have caused frozen water to melt in one or two areas on Earth. Asteroids and comets also had a part to play in making our seas (see page 61).

3,900 MYA: Earth and the Moon finally cool down and settle.

3,900 MYA: the Heavy Bombardment period reaches its peak.

3,800 MYA: the first forms of life begin to appear in Earth's ocean.

3,850 MYA: water vapor in Earth's atmosphere begins to condense, falling as rain. This forms an ocean.

3,500 MYA: bacteria develop primitive forms of photosynthesis.

3) BACTERIAL LIFE FORMS ON EARTH

Bacteria are a group of simple, microscopic single-celled organisms. They were the first life forms to develop on Earth. They eventually evolved into more complex organisms that have DNA. DNA is a complex chemical that carries genetic information from one generation to the next as organisms reproduce.

4) BACTERIA START TO CREATE THEIR OWN FOOD

All of today's organisms evolved from a life form known as the "last universal common ancestor." Two main strands of life branched off from this organism: bacteria and archaea. The bacteria began to use a form of photosynthesis to get food and energy out of sunlight.

5) BACTERIA START TO GIVE OUT OXYGEN

Then came cyanobacteria, which also use photosynthesis to obtain their food energy. A very important difference, however, is that they also produce oxygen (the gas our bodies need) as a byproduct of photosynthesis. This development caused oxygen levels in Earth's atmosphere to rise steadily.

LIFE CHART

3,600 million years of life on Earth: here are some of the highlights . . .

3,800 MYA: Simple cells form

2,000 MYA: Complex cells form

1,000 MYA: Multicellular life begins

600 MYA: Simple animals evolve

550 MYA: Complex animals evolve

500 MYA: Fish and early forms of amphibians evolve

475 MYA: Land plants evolve

400 MYA: Insects and seeds come into being

360 MYA: Amphibians arrive

300 MYA: Reptiles arrive

230 MYA: Dinosaurs (a branch of reptiles) evolve

200 MYA: Mammals arrive

150 MYA: Birds evolve

130 MYA: Flowers come into being

65 MYA: Dinosaurs die out

2.5 MYA: The genus "Homo" (early humans) evolves

0.2 MYA: Humans begin to look a little more like they do today

2,500 MYA: cyanobacteria have evolved.

BIG OBSTACLES

One moment you think your species is doing just fine, enjoying a cozy existence in the early Earth environment. Then—KA-BOOM!! Disaster strikes. And the worst kind of disaster is one that comes from outer space—a big obstacle, such as an asteroid or comet, that smacks into the planet and ruins life as we know it.

THE BIG PROBLEM WITH IMPACTS

Throughout history, impacts have been a big problem for life on Earth. They have had the potential to wipe out life or "interrupt" its development. When Earth was a much younger planet, collisions with large objects were very common—so common, in fact, that today's geologists use the dates of very big impacts to divide and describe the early history of our planet. Fortunately, such collisions are much less common now.

INTERRUPTED EVOLUTION

Change on Earth isn't all slow and gradual. In the past, dramatic events have occurred that have changed the nature of the planet. This means that life has had to change, too. Young Earth collided with another planet to form the Moon, and 65 million years ago, a comet or asteroid hit Earth and caused an extinction (wiped out lots of life). Such events force nature to start again.

Some extraterrestrials pose for a family photo. Meanwhile . . .

. . . CRRRUNCH!! An asteroid collides with their planet.

Asteroids are rocky objects, smaller than planets. In our solar system, most of them are found in the asteroid belt that orbits the Sun between Mars and Jupiter (see page 30).

Comets are balls of ice and dust in orbit around the Sun. They are often visible from Earth when they pass near the Sun, as they develop two "tails." One tail is of dust that reflects the sunlight. The other is glowing gas.

DRAMATIC CHANGES

KNOCK, KNOCK—DELIVERIES FROM SPACE ARRIVING!

Collisions are not always bad news. Asteroids and comets may have seeded our planet with water (H_2O) and carbon-based molecules—both essential ingredients for life—when they crashed into Earth almost four billion years ago. These molecules may have played a key part in the development of life on Earth. This also shows that the basic materials for life can be found elsewhere in space.

THE LAST DAYS OF THE DINOSAURS

The big event that killed the dinosaurs, 65 million years ago, was one in which 75 percent of Earth's species became extinct. Scientists think an asteroid crashed into Earth. The impact would have sent out shock waves and tidal waves, started forest fires, and caused hundreds of thousands of years of severe climate change. Massive volcanic eruptions, happening at the same time, may also have had an effect on the climate.

PLANET EARTH'S BIG EXTINCTION EVENTS

Since life began on Earth, there have been a number of big extinction events. These occur when conditions on Earth have led to a sharp fall in the variety and abundance of life. The most spectacular of these was the time of the "Great Dying," around 252 million years ago. At that time, 96 percent of all marine (ocean-based) species and 70 percent of all land species became extinct (died out). Another very famous extinction, millions and millions of years later, wiped out the dinosaurs.

LIFE MATERIALS

Imagine you have the power to create life—and that you can hurry your creations along a little bit and watch them evolve. What ingredients should you use? If all you had to do was go down to the local shopping mall for the materials, what would they be? And once you had found those vital ingredients, how would you organize them to make life work?

LIFE'S COMMON INGREDIENTS: THE MATTER THAT MATTERS

All things are made of matter, which is composed of tiny particles called atoms. Atoms of different types are called elements. These different atoms can combine to form molecules. Some of the elements that combine to compose living organic matter include carbon, hydrogen, nitrogen, oxygen, phosphorus, sulfur, calcium, and iron.

A RECIPE FOR LIFE: ADD LIQUID AND ENERGY

In order for life to exist on Earth, liquid water is vital. Scientists believe that liquids carry the chemicals of life back and forth. In solids, life can hardly budge. In gases, chemicals are moving around too quickly to react with one another. Besides water, other liquids may host life—such as the ammonia on Enceladus and the methane on Titan (see page 27). Energy is equally essential—about 99 percent of life on Earth needs the Sun's energy in order to function. Earth could exist on its own—but without the Sun, our planet would be lifeless.

ARE THERE OTHER "LIFE RECIPES" OUT THERE?

The elements we find on Earth are the same elements we find in space—carbon, hydrogen, oxygen, and so on. But if these elements are organized into life on other worlds, we are not sure whether the chemical units that provide life's functions will be the same as ours. Will they have DNA? If life is to survive and evolve, it will have to reproduce itself, so life WOULD need a chemical such as DNA to pass genetic information down through the generations of living things.

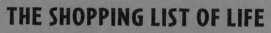

THE SHOPPING LIST OF LIFE

DNA
The chemical in almost all known living organisms that passes information down through the generations.

RNA
A chemical in cells that carries instructions, from DNA, for controlling the production of proteins.

PROTEINS
Complex chemicals created by joining small chemicals called amino acids, made of carbon, hydrogen, oxygen, and nitrogen.

LIPIDS
Chemicals, including fats and some vitamins, whose main life function is to store energy.

OXYGEN
A highly reactive, nonmetallic element that reacts with almost all other elements to form chemicals.

AMMONIA
A gas (made up of the elements hydrogen and nitrogen) that is an important source of nitrogen for living systems.

ENERGY
In living things, energy is responsible for cell growth and development. Energy is often stored by cells in chemicals such as sugars, lipids, and proteins.

SPEEDS OF LIFE

Imagine you're a planet maker. Your planet sits warmly and happily in the Goldilocks zone (see pages 32–33), orbiting its parent star. Your planet has all of the common ingredients for life—or at least those that seem to work on Earth. Using these same ingredients, does life's path always move at the same rate or is it possible to speed up life and enjoy evolution in the fast lane?

HOW QUICKLY DOES LIFE DEVELOP?

It's a tricky question! So far in this book, you've seen that life's path, or evolution, depends on many things. From tiny bacteria to the blue whale, size is certainly a factor. Changes in the environment, such as comet collisions and climate changes, also affect the speed of life—the rate at which living things develop and change.

COULD THERE BE MORE LIFE THAN WE THINK?

Scientists are not certain how many species roam Earth. Their guesses vary from two million to 100 million! If we ignore bacteria, however, our best guess is about ten to 14 million species. But be warned! Experts are still counting, adding thousands of new species each year.

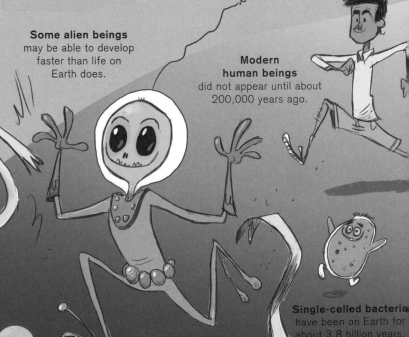

Some alien beings may be able to develop faster than life on Earth does.

Modern human beings did not appear until about 200,000 years ago.

Single-celled bacteria have been on Earth for about 3.8 billion years.

HOW QUICKLY DID HUMANS DEVELOP?

Humans share a common ancestor with chimpanzees, but they started to branch off about 5–7 million years ago. By about 2.5 million years ago, early humans had evolved. Human subspecies, such as Neanderthals, lived alongside our ancestors. Neanderthals lived in Europe about 200,000 years ago, when modern humans first appeared, but died out about 30,000 years ago.

Dinosaurs got knocked out of the life race about 65 million years ago.

The Neanderthals' race is lost . . . and scientists are still trying to explain why they disappeared.

WHAT MAKES A WINNING LIFE FORM?

Consider bacteria. There are more bacteria on Earth than there are humans. They inhabit virtually every environment on the planet, including the soil, water, air, and your body! They have a broader range of species than any other group of organisms. Their activities range from the very useful (such as helping us digest our food) to the not so useful (such as spreading disease).

Crocodilians, a highly successful group of reptiles, have lived on Earth for about 84 million years.

ARE THERE SPEEDIER TYPES OF LIFE OUT THERE IN SPACE?

The main driving force of evolution is natural selection. This is when a species survives only if it develops the right characteristics for its environment. But a species relies on genetic mutation (a permanent change in its DNA) in order to change and adapt. If an alien has DNA that can mutate quickly, it could evolve quickly.

WHAT ALIENS MIGHT LOOK LIKE

BEAUTY IS IN THE EYE OF THE BEHOLDER. What's weird to us is normal to other creatures. Lizards? Dinosaurish. Birds of paradise? Gorgeous. Spiders? Creepy. Humans? Far from perfect. What sort of features might aliens have? What might their chemical makeup be like? On Earth, life is based on carbon and water. On alien worlds, there could be an alien chemistry. The evolution of life might happen under completely different conditions.

ASTROBIOLOGY

Astrobiology is the study of the beginning, evolution, and future of life in the universe. It covers some of the coolest science topics of today, such as looking for life in our solar system, the hunt for other Earths, and the search for clever aliens in deep space. In this book, we have been practicing astrobiology, and these are the questions we have asked so far.

We Have Asked: WHAT IS LIFE?

WHAT exactly IS life? How do we define it? We need an open-minded answer to this question as a starting point so that we can begin to think about life in space. The trouble is, our science of biology is limited to life on Earth. But when we look at all of the weird and wonderful creatures on Earth, we can at least realize how varied and unusual life can be.

We Have Asked: WHERE CAN LIFE EXIST?

WHERE in the universe is life most likely to be found? Thinking big, this leads us to ask, "Where inside a galaxy is life most likely to evolve?" Or, "Where in each system of stars and planets is life most likely to develop and survive?" Once again, the answers to all such big questions are "best guesses" based on our knowledge of life on planet Earth.

Life in space may not be what we expect it to be. We need to be open-minded about life, as it may come in many strange and fascinating forms.

In order to locate life, we must narrow the field. We need to know the most likely places in which life could evolve so that we can quicken the hunt.

THE WIDE WORLD OF ASTROBIOLOGY

The science of astrobiology imaginatively combines a host of different subjects, including astronomy, biology, earth science, and geography. It also has a long history, though it hasn't always been known by the same name. For centuries, many of the world's greatest scholars have wondered whether there is life way out in the blackness of space.

We Have Asked: WHEN DID LIFE GET GOING?

WHEN in the history of the universe was life most likely to happen? If life began early in time, any early alien civilizations—if they have survived— might be highly evolved and extremely sophisticated. They may be capable of space travel and very long lives. If life in the universe began later, alien civilizations may not be any more advanced than we are.

We Have Asked: HOW DOES LIFE BEGIN?

HOW would life begin to form in the universe? This would depend on the place and time. It would also depend on the type of materials available in the local environment. They may not be the same kinds of materials from which life develops on Earth. Once life is under way, how quickly will things develop and evolve? The speeds of life may vary greatly.

We need to figure out the timeline of life. If life started early on in the history of the universe, aliens may be highly evolved and smart.

We need to know all about the building blocks that make life. Are these starting materials the same throughout the vast, vast universe?

EVOLUTION ON EARTH

The basic idea behind evolution is that all species have evolved from simple life forms. Simple life started on this planet about 3.8 billion years ago. A series of changes in life's path on Earth meant that these organisms developed from the first bacteria all the way through to the first "modern" humans.

★ IS EVOLUTION LIKE A LADDER?

One way of looking at evolution is to picture it in the form of a ladder: time's ladder. In many books and charts, the changes in life's path on Earth, plotted over time, are represented as rungs on the ladder—rungs such as Age of Reptiles, Age of Mammals, Age of Man and so on. But, in fact, a ladder is not the best way of expressing how evolution works.

★ TREEVOLUTION

The ladder model actually gives a false impression of how life changes and varies on Earth. We now tend to look at life's path as a "tree" of evolution, or "treevolution"! The tree model, illustrated here, shows that all life on Earth is related, with branches indicating how life diversifies naturally (becomes more varied) over time.

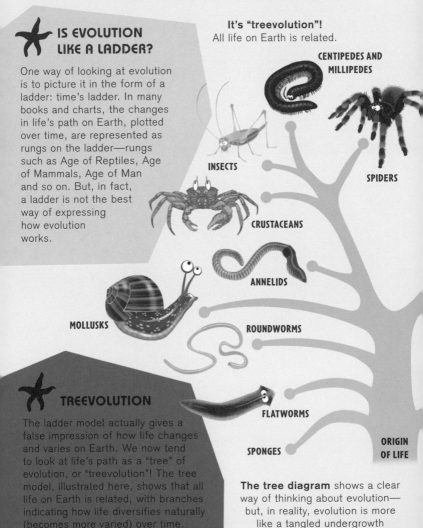

It's "treevolution"!
All life on Earth is related.

CENTIPEDES AND MILLIPEDES

SPIDERS

INSECTS

CRUSTACEANS

ANNELIDS

MOLLUSKS

ROUNDWORMS

FLATWORMS

SPONGES

ORIGIN OF LIFE

The tree diagram shows a clear way of thinking about evolution—but, in reality, evolution is more like a tangled undergrowth than a nice, neat tree.

WALLACE AND DARWIN

Alfred Russel Wallace and Charles Darwin developed the theory of natural selection. Darwin stated that competition between individuals of the same species is important for them to survive. Wallace's theory said that environmental pressures on species are also important, as they force animals to adapt to their natural habitats (see pages 74–75).

Charles Darwin
(1809–1882)

Alfred Russel Wallace
(1823–1913)

MAMMALS
(including humans)

BIRDS

REPTILES

AMPHIBIANS

TUNICATES

FISH

ECHINODERMS

CNIDARIANS

The branches on this tree show examples of life that STILL exist on Earth.

⭐ THE THEORY OF NATURAL SELECTION

A good explanation for how evolution works is the theory of natural selection (see above). This theory says that individual members of a species that are well adapted to their environments are more likely to survive and reproduce. This means that their genes and characteristics are more likely to be passed on to the next generation. So, if given enough time to do so, a species will gradually evolve.

It is important to remember that most of the species that evolved on Earth are now extinct.

⭐ BUT TREAT THE TREE WITH CAUTION!

The tree of evolution is a handy way of showing how life branches out and becomes more varied as time goes by. But it has its drawbacks. It suggests that evolution is a straight progression from simple to complex life, inferior to superior, and with mammals (our animal group) at the top. The tree also focuses mostly on organisms that are still alive. The vast majority of Earth's organisms are extinct (having no more living relatives).

C◖◗SMIC CARB◖◗N

Carbon forms the basis of life on Earth, but it is also found way out in deep space. It is the "backbone" (main support) of biology because it bonds easily with life's other main elements—such as hydrogen, oxygen, and nitrogen—to make other substances. Carbon is also very light and small, making it an ideal element for creating complex chemicals of life such as proteins and DNA that are made up of long chains of molecules.

CARBON'S COSMIC CHEMISTRY

So what makes carbon so cosmic? Think about its variety. It makes one of the softest known substances— called graphite—and also one of the hardest known materials—diamond! In all, carbon is known to form ten million different chemicals, which is the majority of all of the chemicals on planet Earth. Now that's cosmic!

CARBON OUT IN SPACE

Carbon is made in the cores of giant and supergiant stars (the most massive stars). It is then scattered into space as dust in supernova explosions. Some stars use carbon as a catalyst for their fiery fusion reactions (see page 15). Also, a number of complex carbon chemicals have been found in space, including sugar!

Silicon-based trees loom over this fantastical silicon-rich world.

Silicon-based life forms might evolve in places where carbon is not plentiful enough to form the basis of life's chemistry.

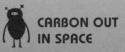

ARE THERE OTHER LIFE MATERIALS?

Carbon combines with hydrogen, oxygen, and nitrogen to make life's complex chemicals. Its chemistry has the ability to form the long "hydrocarbon chains" of life. Silicon is an element in the same chemical group as carbon. So, in theory, there may be places out in space where nature uses silicon as a basis for the chemistry of life rather than carbon.

NONCARBON CREATURES

Most scientists believe that alien life will also be carbon based. But some say this is very narrow-minded and that noncarbon creatures might evolve from other elements in an environment that is not rich in carbon. Science-fiction writers have already imagined "silicon spiders," for example.

SUPER SOLVENTS!

NEW!!! LIQUID LIFE JUICE

Life on Earth is carbon based and water based. Water acts as a solvent, dissolving molecules (chemicals with two or more atoms) and allowing them to reassemble in ways suitable for life. But might alien life use another solvent? NASA scientists have suggested liquid ammonia and methane as possible alternatives. Methane is an exciting prospect, as there are huge lakes of liquid methane on Saturn's largest moon, Titan.

Silicon spiders climb the stalks in this dry silicon desert.

COULD A SILICON LIFE FORM EXIST?

The important chemical processes of life, such as respiration and photosynthesis, would not work without carbon. But we know this to be true only of life on Earth. Life in space might use different processes. However, one thing is worth remembering: there is a lot more silicon on Earth than carbon, yet nature still chooses carbon as its favorite material for building living organisms.

FITTING IN

Every organism lives in a unique ecosystem, its natural habitat. This habitat provides the organism's basic needs—food, water, shelter, and so on. All organisms need to adapt to their environment in order to survive: this means adapting to be able to avoid predators, survive the conditions of the climate, and compete with other species for the same food and space.

FITTING IN WITH THE ENVIRONMENT

Polar bear hairs are hollow tubes that reflect sunlight, making the animals' fur appear white. So, besides keeping them warm, the fur hides them against a snowy background. Camels are well adapted to a hot climate, as they can go for a long time without water and have two rows of eyelashes to keep out sand. As their environment changes, creatures need to keep adapting to be able to survive in it.

SPACE AND SIZE

Did you know that the ancestor of the enormous dodo was a normal-sized pigeon? Animals get big when their environment lacks the usual predators. This happens a lot on isolated islands. The opposite can also happen: small animals sometimes evolve when their population is limited to a small environment, such as an island.

These small rodents (below) have a different diet from the big dinosaur, so they are not competing for the same food.

Sauropods had extremely long necks. This adaptation gave them access to a greater range of vegetation.

Large sauropod dinosaurs existed on Earth around 210–65 million years ago.

OUR THEORIES ABOUT DINOSAUR SIZE

The sauropods were herbivores (plant eaters), and some of them grew to a gargantuan size. Some say they grew so big because they ate so much vegetation. Others say it was because they wanted to deter predators from eating them. If dinosaurs were cold-blooded (and we still don't know if they were), they would have used much more of their food energy for growth rather than for staying warm. So that's another possible reason.

Plants also compete with one another, especially for the Sun's light and minerals in the soil.

FITTING IN TOGETHER

Sometimes organisms adapt in a way that offers benefits to other organisms. Cows and horses are both good examples. Cows' intestines are packed with bacteria that help them digest food. Meanwhile, the bacteria benefit from nutrients inside the cow. Humans domesticate horses so that they can perform jobs. But the horses benefit from this relationship, too, as they are fed, groomed, cared for, and kept safe from predators.

THE BIOLOGICAL EVOLUTION OF ALIENS

Humans adapted and evolved from lobe-finned fish (see page 22). In time, we developed two arms, two legs, hair and so on. Real aliens will not look like us. Lobe-finned fish are unlikely to be among their ancestors. But some of our features may also crop up on other worlds. Brains, eyes, mouths, and jointed limbs may prove useful for adaptation on other moons and planets, too.

75

BODY PATTERNS

Does nature have a secret "favorites" file, hidden away in its systems? Does nature prefer certain patterns and trends to others? Why do animals often have two eyes, ears, arms, and nostrils, for instance? This balanced organization of body parts or shapes is known as symmetry.

SYMMETRY IN NATURE

The body plans of most complex creatures have symmetry. When an organism can be divided into right and left halves that are a mirror image of each other, this is known as bilateral symmetry. When an organism is equally spaced around a central point like spokes on a wheel, this is called radial symmetry. Species with no symmetry are asymmetrical.

IS SYMMETRY IN GENES?

When scientists carry out experiments to find out how symmetry works in nature, they get some surprising results. Symmetry is not easily "broken." Genetic tests have been carried out on a species of fruit fly. Scientists were able to change certain fruit fly features, such as its body shape, but they were not able to change the fly's overall symmetry. It still had the same arrangement of limbs, wings, and so on. Experiments such as this suggest that symmetry is deeply coded in the genes of plants and animals.

Porifera sponges are a type of life form on Earth that show no symmetry.

Can you tell which of these tiny plankton (above) have bilateral symmetry and which have radial symmetry?

These sponges rely on the flow of water through their porous (holey) bodies for food and oxygen.

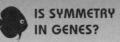

76

IS SYMMETRY ALWAYS IN FASHION?

Researchers are not really sure whether alien life forms would display symmetry. Aliens might actually show asymmetry, depending on the conditions of their evolution and environment. On Earth, there are some asymmetrical creatures. Porifera sponges (below) have no symmetry. There are also about 400 species of flatfish that develop into an asymmetrical shape: they start off with an eye on each side of the body, but one eye moves to the other side, along with their mouth and jaws, as they grow into adulthood.

ATTACK OF THE TRIPODS!

In "The War of the Worlds", by H. G. Wells, the aliens are octopus-like creatures, and their spacecraft walk on three legs, with metallic tentacles underneath. Real aliens wouldn't be like us because their body plan isn't based on the lobe-finned fish that came ashore many years ago on Earth (see page 22). But some aliens might have exoskeletons (outside skeletons), move around on wheels, or even have electric limbs!

Adult flatfish can feed on the ocean floor while looking upward as both of their eyes end up on the same side.

REPEATING FASHIONS IN EVOLUTION

Sometimes the process of evolution repeats certain features over the course of time. Convergent evolution happens when unrelated organisms evolve similar bodily features as a result of having to adapt to the same kind of environment. The wing is a very good example. Bats and birds are both capable of flight using wings. They are not related, but they have a common ancestor. This ancestor did not have wings, but bats and birds both developed wings by adapting the body shape that this common relative had.

77

 SUPER SENSES

Humans experience life through five main senses—we see, hear, smell, touch, and taste. These senses are better developed in some animals, and some organisms are able to sense the world in ways that humans cannot. By studying these senses, we can consider the sort of senses that aliens may have. This knowledge might help us communicate with them.

SEEING SENSE

A scavenging vulture can spy a carcass (dead body) from great distances. A four-eyed fish can see above and below the water at the same time. A fly's compound eye is made up of hundreds of tiny six-sided lenses packed together like a honeycomb. Other creatures can see in the ultraviolet spectrum of light. Might aliens have super-vision, too?

Four-eyed fish can see two worlds—one airy, one watery.

Migrating birds use Earth's magnetic field to find their way.

GOOD SENSE OF TIMING

The cycles of the Moon and Sun are the rhythms that govern life on Earth, creating days, nights, and seasons. But an animal's perception of time also varies according to its heart rate. A shrew's heart beats up to 20 times faster than a human's, so time appears to pass more slowly. Likewise, an alien may experience time differently.

A shrew's heartbeat can reach 1,200 beats per minute (bpm), compared with 60 bpm for humans.

MAKING SENSE OF THE WORLD

Animals experience the world through a combination of different senses. Their minds create cognitive maps to aid their navigation around the planet. Other senses have evolved owing to the need to hunt for food or to avoid being eaten. An intelligent alien would also use a full set of senses to survive and communicate.

UNSEEN SENSES

Earth-based animals also use senses that are hidden to humans. Sensitivity to Earth's electromagnetic fields can be used to aid navigation. Other creatures can predict earthquakes. Predators put these senses to lethal use: a shark homes in on the body electricity of its prey. Aliens could have similar abilities.

SOUND SENSES

Our ears have a limited range. We're deaf to low-pitched elephant chatter and to the high-pitched squeaks of mice. Whales use sonar (sound pulses) to communicate across hundreds of miles of water, while spiders listen for the wing beats of their prey. The kangaroo rat also has very sensitive hearing.

Some snakes can sense the body heat of their prey.

Whale music (available here on CD) can also be used in locating their prey.

These two aliens exchange thoughts on whether or not to buy the album of whale music on CD.

The springbok's alarm odor says, "Smell this, my friends—trouble is coming!"

SUPER SCENTS

Smelling is vital in hunting, navigation, and self-defense. The petrel (a sea bird) uses its fantastic sense of smell to find fish in the open ocean. The springbok (a type of gazelle, above) emits an "alarm" odor to warn its herd of a predator. A salmon's journey across the ocean, simply to lay eggs, is also achieved through its sense of smell.

SENSING THOUGHTS

Could aliens talk to each other telepathically, using their thoughts? Well, there's nothing like it on Earth. The most similar ability is the shark's electrosense (see above). But telepathy would need brains that are programmed exactly alike, and evolution doesn't seem to work in this way.

HOW TO TALK TO ALIENS

HOW DO WE STAY IN TOUCH WITH OUTER SPACE? Have any of our messages to the Great Unknown been answered? And if we do meet aliens, how will we talk to them? This chapter attempts to answer such questions by thinking about how we became intelligent, the different ways in which we communicate, and how we first created language. So let's stay in contact with the cosmos and see what happens!

GETTING CLEVER

Intelligence is the ability to learn things and develop skills and to apply that learning to different situations. Intelligence seems to be something that separates us from many other animals, but is it really all that useful? Can life forms evolve WITHOUT intelligence? If it IS useful and necessary how do some species become more intelligent than others?

Stone Age tools

A TIMELINE OF HUMAN INTELLIGENCE

Fire being used to cook food and stay warm

Tarpan wild horse, from the Eurasian steppes (between Europe and Asia)

2.9 million years ago: the earliest known stone tools

2.5 million years ago: the genus Homo (early humans) evolves

300,000–400,000 years ago: evidence of the controlled use of fire

200,000 years ago: modern human beings evolve

30,000 years ago: the earliest known pottery and artifacts

10,000 years ago: the first human settlements

6,000 years ago: horses are tamed by humans

DOES EVOLUTION LEAD TO INTELLIGENCE?

It's not easy to compare human intelligence with that of other animals. Animals do not normally read or write, so it can be difficult to measure how smart they are. But intelligence has cropped up on numerous branches of Earth's tree of life (see pages 70–71). Mantis shrimp, octopuses, whales, dolphins, and apes—all of these display the ability to learn things and apply skills.

ARE ALL SUCCESSFUL SPECIES INTELLIGENT?

To us, it seems that humans are the most successful species, due to our unique intelligence. But what about bacteria? They're not smart, and yet they have been remarkably successful on Earth: they've been around for as many as 3.8 billion years, and they are present almost everywhere on the planet. On average just 0.04 oz. (1g) of soil contains about 40 million bacterial cells.

NASA's lunar excursion module (LEM)—used to make six crewed landings on the Moon (1969-1972)

Optical telescope from the early 1600s

Stone wheel

Stylus (writing tool) and clay tablet

International Space Station (ISS)—under construction since 1998

5,000 years ago: the invention of writing

In around 1608: the invention of the telescope

July 21, 1969: humans walk on the Moon

5,500 years ago: the invention of the wheel

In around 1440: the invention of the printing press

April 12, 1961: a human being travels into space

2000 onward: humans have a constant presence in Earth's orbit

HOW DID HUMANS GET SO CLEVER?

All species fight for space and food, but evolution is not all about competition. Humans have thrived through cooperation. Early humans developed skills such as the use of tools—but the key development was the way they began to interact with one another. They learned how to communicate, and this would have been an essential step on the road to "Team Human" (see page 84).

IS INTELLIGENCE DUE TO THE SIZE OF OUR BRAINS?

Not necessarily. Brain size usually increases with body size in animals. Larger animals tend to have larger brains, as they need them to control their big bodies. The way in which animals train their brains as they evolve is probably more important. The size of a modern human's brain is like that of an ancient human's, but the difference in learning, skills, and ability is huge!

TEAM HUMAN!

Now that we've seen the history of human intelligence, let's look at the lives of early people. We've seen that human evolution can lead to major breakthroughs that change the way in which society works. But how do these breakthroughs come about? And what do we know about how these changes work?

THE OPPOSABLE THUMB: USING TOOLS

Evolution provided us with a major advantage over other animals. We developed the "opposable thumb"—a thumb that can be moved around opposite the fingers of the same hand so that we can grab things. Many other animals have also developed this type of thumb. In humans, the opposable thumb has allowed us to hold things in our hands, such as tools, and control them more skillfully.

Humans managed to adapt to a colder climate during the Ice Age, which reached its peak around 20,000 years ago and ended around 11,500 years ago.

Wielding tools during a hunt is much easier with an opposable thumb!

HUNTING AND GATHERING

A hunter-gatherer community is one where the food is either gathered from wild plants or hunted from wild animals. Human society was like this up until settled farming began around 10,000 years ago. Early humans gathered seafood, eggs, nuts, and fruits and only later learned how to hunt. And to hunt, they needed to cooperate as Team Human!

Woolly mammoths existed on Earth between about 150,000 and 10,000 years ago.

A SETTLED EXISTENCE

During the Neolithic agricultural revolution, as early as 10,000 years ago, there was a change to a more settled existence. In certain parts of the world, a new farming lifestyle was developing, which meant society was now based in villages and towns. Creating a lot of food from farming led to the development of a more complex society in which foods and goods were exchanged between people.

HUNTERS AND FARMERS: WHICH DID BETTER?

A regular food supply actually made humans worse off. Hunter-gatherers had a more varied diet, better health, and an average height of 5 ft. 8 in. (173cm). But after the Neolithic agricultural revolution, the average height went down to 5 ft. 3 in. (160cm)—and human height did not get back to normal until the 1900s. Early farmers also had shorter lives, which is partly due to the diseases they began to suffer.

HUMAN BEINGS: THE DREAM TEAM!

After the agricultural revolution, humans had to get organized. The development of bigger societies meant people now had different kinds of jobs. It also meant that decision making changed. Humans had to learn to communicate, operate better as a team, and share tasks. This stage in our history was a major step forward on the path to becoming such a dominant species.

The ability to control fire led to cooked food and a more varied diet. It was also useful for scaring beasts!

BODY SIGNALS

We are now ready to think about how a common language grows between creatures of the same species. We might also wonder whether it's possible to have a common language between different species. If there are any alien civilizations out there, how do these creatures go about making their needs known? How did they learn to work together as a group?

These birdlike creatures display their colorful crests and body parts to attract a mate.

Courtship dance is an important way for animals and humans to show that they are ready to find a mate for producing offspring.

RITUAL DANCE

On this planet, people and animals take part in ritual behavior at certain times of the year to celebrate a festival, the changing of the seasons, or for religious reasons. This may involve movement and dance, which are important forms of communication. Aliens may also take part in ritual and ceremonial types of behavior.

EXOTIC DISPLAY

Animals can be very cunning about the way they present themselves to others. Physical features can be enhanced: bold colors and markings help warn off predators, and an attractive crest or feathers may help tempt a mate or show superiority in a group. Some animals also protect themselves from predators by making their bodies look much bigger than they actually are.

FACIAL SIGNALS

A creature's face is a very sophisticated way of displaying moods, emotions, desires, and responses to events. All organisms react to things. If they didn't, they would not survive! A lot of facial expressions are involuntary: the facial muscles react automatically to show an emotion. But animals and humans can also control their expressions to deliberately mislead and deceive others.

Vocal sounds are also used to attract attention.

Gestures and expressions are very fast and efficient ways of communicating a feeling or a point of view.

VOCAL SOUNDS AND LANGUAGE

How does language develop? Scientists think that vocal forms of communication—in humans, birds, whales, and other animals—may have started with music and song or perhaps with simple but repeated sounds that got ideas or messages across. These primitive noises then led to a recognized sequence of sounds that slowly gathered meaning.

CREATING LANGUAGE

How did our spoken words develop and how might they develop on other worlds? The origin of language is shrouded in mystery. Even though it is a hot topic, there is little agreement between scientists on the origin or age of language in either its written or spoken forms. Finding the proof is tricky.

Cave paintings found in Chauvet, France, may be 30,000–35,000 years old, while those found in Nerja, Spain, could be 43,500 years old.

CREATURES WITH A "VOICE"

Some scientists study wild apes to figure out how language works. Apes make a range of sounds, but their anatomy (body structure) does not enable them to make many of the sounds that modern humans do. As humans began to walk upright, important changes may have occurred inside their skulls, allowing speech to develop.

Horses feature regularly in Upper Paleolithic cave art.

RELATING IDEAS TO VOCAL SOUNDS

When human infants learn to speak, they learn by example. They pick up spoken words by identifying the vocal sounds that are used for different objects and ideas. They mostly do this by copying other people, such as their parents, and they start by learning about the objects that are related to their most basic needs. Eating, drinking, and sleeping are the main needs of any young creature.

These animal artworks might represent some kind of spell—cast to bring about successful hunting.

COMMON ROCK SCRIBBLES

Types of spiritual or religious activities can be seen in some rock and cave paintings (see below).

Scientists have begun to research the marks that appear around the edges of rock or cave art. There are 26 signs altogether, all drawn in the same style that appear again and again at many sites. Some are basic, involving straight lines and circles and triangles, but even so, they may be meaningful. They could even be the seeds of written communication.

THE LANGUAGE OF GROUP ACTIVITIES

It could be that a "vocabulary" (a range of words used in a language) developed from the activities of a community of people, such as hunters (see pages 84–85). As people began to live together in groups, they must have started to agree on certain ways of expressing ideas and labeling things, using their voices.

THE LANGUAGE OF ROCK AND CAVE ART

Experts believe our ancestors had a "creative explosion" in Europe from as early as 43,500 years ago. Humans suddenly began to think creatively and produce art in a period known as the Upper Paleolithic (c. 40,000–10,000 years ago). There's plenty of evidence for this in the stunning cave paintings that can still be seen across Europe.

The **"penniform" sign** often appears next to animal images, so it may mean "arrow" or "spear."

The **"spiral" symbol** is quite a common shape in nature, so its symbolism is a mystery

The **"crosshatch"** is another example of a symbol found at sites all over the world.

The **"claviform" sign** looks like the numeral "1," but it might also stand for "woman."

Some signs are grouped together to express a particular meaning or idea.

MAKING CONTACT

How will we communicate with aliens across the gulf of space? Will they understand us? And what have we tried so far? By studying the common aspects of Earthly languages, scientists hope to understand how we might talk to extraterrestrials. So if we get a signal from space, we'll be ready to chat!

USING SIGNS TO MAKE CONTACT

In the 1820s, German mathematician Carl Friedrich Gauss (1777–1855) tried to contact aliens by reflecting sunlight toward planets. He also suggested cutting a forest into the shape of a mathematical diagram to show aliens that we are intelligent. An Austrian astronomer named Joseph von Littrow (1781–1840) wanted to signal to aliens by digging trenches in the Sahara Desert to form various shapes. The trenches were to be filled with fuel and set on fire.

Huge radio telescopes on Earth listen for signals from deep space.

"Brrring-brrring!!" One day, maybe an alien race will attempt to communicate a message of great importance to our future on Earth.

SCANNING THE SKIES FOR INTELLIGENCE

The Search for Extraterrestrial Intelligence, or SETI, is the name of a sophisticated project that looks for intelligent life in space. SETI technicians use radio telescopes to scan parts of space for evidence of signals from unknown objects or places on other worlds. They have begun to target the space around the stars where habitable worlds may lie.

A POSTCARD FROM OUTER SPACE

IT'S A MESSAGE FROM AN ALIEN RACE!
Or is it..? See if you can decipher it, and
then check out the solutions on page 105.

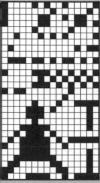

One of the most famous message
puzzles ever created is this one, shown
on the left. It was designed by a SETI
scientist named Frank Drake. The message
is supposed to be from an alien race to us.
The message is complex and difficult to
decode, so a simplified version is shown on
the right. Using the simpler message, see
if you can figure out what the different
parts of it mean. A good way to begin is
to find something you recognize and go
from there. Remember . . . in science,
all guesses are good guesses!

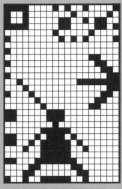

ANK DRAKE'S MESSAGE

THE SIMPLIFIED MESSAGE

LINCOS: A LANGUAGE OF RADIO SIGNALS

Lincos—short for lingua cosmica,
meaning "universal language"—is a
made-up language designed to be
understood by intelligent aliens. It was
developed by Dr. Hans Freudenthal in
1960. Lincos uses a simple pattern
of radio signals that acts as a
dictionary to communicate simple
or complex messages.

SCI-FI SPEAK AND OTHER "FUTURE" LANGUAGES

Writers sometimes try to invent an
alien language to make the world
of their stories more believable. The
most famous example is Klingon,
a language based on the fictional
Klingon aliens in "Star Trek", a U.S.
sci-fi TV series. Fans of the show
can even take lessons to learn this
alien language for themselves!

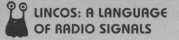

BEFORE YOU READ THIS CHAPTER, YOU MUST CARRY OUT A SIMPLE SCIENCE EXPERIMENT. Stop thinking of yourself as a human and start thinking of yourself as a curious creature from outer space. Because to other life forms out there, that's what you are! Our final chapter considers alien technology, alien visits, and the idea of humans as aliens. Did we come from somewhere else? And will we one day roam the universe as aliens?

ALIEN GADGETS

It would be great to know what kind of gadgets aliens have. They might zip around using personal jetpacks and have mini TVs in their contact lenses. They may have found a way to sneak from one universe to another or travel through time. If we think logically about it, we can try to imagine what alien technology might be like.

ARE ALIENS SMARTER THAN WE ARE?

Well, if they are screaming across the sky in swift and nimble spaceships, perhaps they ARE smarter than us! But it depends on how ancient their civilization is and how speedy their evolution has been. If they've been around for billions of years, you can only imagine how advanced they may be. Humans have become technologically advanced in the past 100 years or so.

Types of cosmic energy and radiation may have been harnessed by aliens for communication. We humans have done the same.

Natural weather conditions might be used to power vehicles, as they are on planet Earth.

A "MIRROR" OF OUR TECHNOLOGY

Some people claim to have seen alien technology when they were abducted and taken onboard a spaceship (see page 97)—or so they say. The trouble is, a lot of the technology that these people have described sounds very similar to gadgets from Earth. In the mid-1900s, aliens had black-and-white TVs, it seems. Then they had PCs and later on MP3 players . . . So our ideas about alien technology seem to be a reflection of our own technological advances!

This alien planet receives starlight only on one side, but a system of mirrors reflects the light over to the other side, too!

ADVANCED SOLAR ENERGY

Some science-fiction writers have been much better at imagining alien technology than scientists. In his 1937 book "Star Maker", British author Olaf Stapledon came up with the idea of a system of orbiting satellites around a star that would capture almost all of the star's energy output. A physicist and mathematician named Freeman Dyson further developed this concept in 1960, which is why the system is now known as a "Dyson sphere."

ARTHUR C. CLARKE

Arthur C. Clarke (1917–2008) was a well-known British science-fiction writer. He wrote "2001: A Space Odyssey", one of the most famous stories about alien contact. Clarke was aware that alien technology might appear very strange to us. He said that any technology that was very advanced would seem "like magic" to human beings.

NECESSITY INSPIRES INVENTION

Our guesses about alien technology should be based on need. Think about the tools we've created on Earth—even primitive ones, such as the wheel. We invented the wheel because we needed to more easily move ourselves and our stuff to other places. So if there is a race of aliens living on a world of water, for example, a lot of their machines will be geared toward sea travel and underwater living.

The strings on this amazing guitar are made from the hairs of some exotic alien creature.

Aliens with many nimble limbs might have tremendous musical instruments.

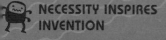

ALIEN VISITS

When we think about human contact with aliens, we often think that aliens might be dangerous. Will they bring war? Will they bring strange diseases? Will they come to take the world for themselves and make us into their slaves? But perhaps aliens are nice, kind, lovable creatures from afar . . . with wonderful gadgets and spaceships!

Aliens might be kind and may come to Earth with exotic gifts.

Aliens might know lots of amazing things they could teach us about.

Aliens might keep other creatures as pets—like we do.

WHY HAVEN'T ALIENS VISITED US YET?

It's an interesting question. If there are intelligent aliens out there with curious natures, why haven't they made contact? One answer may be that, like us, they still find it tricky to travel through space, as the universe is so enormous. Trips into space are dangerous and very expensive.

OR HAVE THEY ALREADY VISITED EARTH?

When you think about alien contact, it's not only the future you should be thinking about. The universe is a very old place, so some alien races could be ancient. Their visit may have happened long ago, before the first humans had even appeared on Earth. Or maybe they liked Earth so much . . . that they decided to stay here!

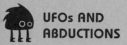

UFOs AND ABDUCTIONS

Some people are convinced that aliens are here on Earth. They report seeing UFOs (unidentified flying objects) in the sky. Some even claim to have been abducted by aliens and taken up into their spaceships. Others believe there are scientific explanations for these events and that tricks of the light and mind are to blame.

HOW WOULD THE WORLD CHANGE?

What would happen if aliens came to Earth? If they were intelligent aliens they would be careful not to bring diseases with them, and their superior spaceship technology would be a wonder to Earth-based scientists. And we would know, at last, that we are not alone in the universe. Of course, if the aliens were unfriendly that would change the situation!

WHAT DOES SCI-FI TEACH US ABOUT ALIENS?

DO: TRY TO HELP THEM OUT

In Steven Spielberg's science-fiction movie "E.T.", a boy named Elliott helps a lost alien find his way home, with a little help from his friends.

DON'T: POINT A WEAPON AT THEM

It would be very bad manners if aliens had come all that way across space just to be offended. Besides, they may have bigger weapons.

DO: SNEEZE ON THEM AND GIVE THEM YOUR GERMS

If aliens ARE nasty, don't hesitate to try all of the tricks in the book. That includes sneezing on them. They may not be able to survive our sneezes and coughs!

DO: KEEP YOUR WITS ABOUT YOU AT ALL TIMES

They may be those sly, shape-shifting aliens, so beware. If so, they could morph into the appearance of the family cat, your grandma, or even your mom!

ARE WE ALIENS?

Yes, we are! If there are aliens out there, we, too, are "alien" to them. But did humans and all life on Earth actually come from somewhere else in space? Flowers are pollinated when they receive pollen grains, allowing them to reproduce. Maybe the "seeds of life," like pollen, have traveled through the universe in a similar way.

DID LIFE GROW FROM ALIEN "SEEDS"?

"Panspermia" is a Greek word that means "seeds everywhere," and it is also the name of a theory. The theory states that there are "seeds of life" all over the universe that can be spread from place to place by traveling bodies such as meteoroids and asteroids. Providing that the life seeds meet with ideal conditions on a new moon or planet, evolution can begin and life forms develop.

HOW THE "SEEDING" MIGHT HAPPEN

Following a collision with a large object, rocks from a planet's surface could be thrown into space. These rocks could then become "transfer vehicles" for spreading biological material from one planet to another or from one planetary system to another. Or the seeds could be transported by an advanced alien civilization.

IS THERE ANY EVIDENCE FOR PANSPERMIA?

In 1984, a team of scientists in Antarctica discovered a meteorite that had been blasted off from the surface of Mars about 15 million years ago. In 1996, tests showed that the meteorite might contain the remains of bacteria. But most experts now agree that the remains are not a definite indication of living matter. The debate goes on!

DOES THIS MEAN THAT ALL LIFE BEGAN IN ONE PLACE?

The panspermia theory does not state that all life came from only one place, at one time, and then spread throughout the entire universe. Yes, if biological life traveled to us on ejected rocks from Mars, it is possible that the Martian life seeds made it to other worlds, too. But this same kind of process could be happening all over the universe, involving different types of life seeds and completely different forms of life.

These aliens are putting on their "human suits" . . . but are they already related to us?

PANSPERMIA IN SCIENCE FICTION

The theory of panspermia was used in "Star Trek", the U.S. TV series, to explain why the aliens were humanoid (humanlike) in appearance. Specially encoded bacteria seeds were spread across the fictional galaxy, billions of years ago, by an ancient race of aliens. On all planets where the seeds landed–hey, presto– humanlike creatures evolved.

IF PANSPERMIA IS TRUE, WHY IS LIFE SO VARIED?

Panspermia is a theory about how life starts and where the raw material comes from. It doesn't change anything else about how life develops, evolves, and diversifies on Earth. The theory suggests that the chemical "trigger" for life came from space rather than Earth, but evolution still has its part to play.

BECOMING ALIENS . . .

Humans are always on the move. The early human species appeared on Earth about 2.5 million years ago, and since then, we haven't sat still, populating the globe. We've even been into orbit and set foot on the Moon. And although we've only just begun to explore space, our robotic probes are already making their way to other stars.

A "human ark" might be used to take entire generations of humans to other worlds in the future.

Generation starships might look like this one. They would need to be huge, and their journeys into deep space could take centuries.

ONE DAY WE MAY BE MARTIANS

Scientists have been predicting and planning our conquest of the solar system for centuries. The Moon is merely the first steppingstone to other worlds. Our next target is a mission to Mars. Space agencies have been training astronauts for the long journey to the Red Planet so that we can set up a colony there. The trip, which will probably take well over 200 days, will be mentally and physically challenging and very dangerous.

IS EXPLORATION A NATURAL URGE?

Are aliens like the Vikings, who left Scandinavia in the late 700s and settled in new lands? Humans seem to have ants in their pants. We are an intelligent and curious species that likes to roam and explore far and wide. But will all intelligent species be like us? Maybe this urge to observe is a key to survival. As history has shown, the creatures that wander and explore tend to increase their chances of survival on this planet.

We'd have to take our natural resources with us until we found an alternative planet to settle on.

Mobile Earth vegetation could be kept inside a portable biosphere—an artificial structure with a self-contained ecosystem.

Experiments in Earth's orbit will teach us how to grow food in space for such long journeys.

ARE ALIENS HAPPY WHERE THEY ARE?

We have seen many changes in the way in which we live. We have developed farming and industry, and maybe we think this is the only kind of progress that will happen to an intelligent species. But what if aliens are perfectly happy living a simple life, gathering food to eat? If so, they'd have no need to roam farther afield.

THE NEED FOR MORE NATURAL RESOURCES

But if aliens are like us, they may be using up all of their land, water, fuel, minerals, forests, and so on. Then they may need to travel into space in search of more supplies. They may have a growing population, as we do, and need to search for resources to feed, clothe, and care for them all.

ALIEN ASTRONOMERS

Picture a planet of alien stargazers. They are happy to stay on their little planet, but they are curious . . . For them, space travel is too tricky and hazardous, so they merely gaze into space. Now picture another planet, where the aliens can't sit still. They simply must roam the universe forever. That's us, on planet Earth!

PUT IT INTO PRACTICE!

GET OUT THERE AND TAKE A LOOK! Science is all about asking questions. Yes, it's important to listen to the big brainiacs, but they are not always correct, and it's important to make up your own mind, too. An easy way to begin your studies is by looking at the night sky. Get ahold of a telescope or a pair of binoculars,or join your local astronomy club. This short chapter includes some alien-hunting projects that you should also look out for.

FINDING LIFE: THE MISSIONS

Astrobiology is one of the most exciting and fastest-developing fields of science. Scientists are researching extreme ecosystems on Earth to see how successfully life can develop in more challenging places. They are also planning missions to Mars and the planetary systems of Jupiter and Saturn. Here's a guide to what is happening and how you can keep up.

VISIT NASA'S ASTROBIOLOGY INSTITUTE

NASA's Astrobiology Institute was set up in 1998 to develop astrobiology and to research the science needed for crewed missions into space.

• WEB LINK •
http://astrobiology.nasa.gov/nai

STUDY THE EARTH SIMILARITY INDEX

Scientists have been making a list of the most habitable worlds. This list is bound to keep growing and growing, so check up on it regularly!

• WEB LINK •
http://timeforkids.com/news/anybody-out-there/21456

NEWS ON THE MOONS: WHAT'S THE LATEST?

Check for updates on the possibility of life on the icy moons of our solar system, such as Titan, Callisto, Enceladus, Europa, and Ganymede.

• WEB LINK •
http://solarsystem.nasa.gov/planets/index.cfm

FIND OUT WHAT'S GOING ON AT NASA

NASA is always planning stuff that will one day take us to new worlds. You can follow the progress of their experiments on Twitter, for example, and on their homepage.

• WEB LINK •
www.nasa.gov

FOLLOW THE KEPLER MISSION

The Kepler space observatory is looking at distant stars that might have habitable worlds in orbit around them. Keep tabs on the mission to see how many Earth-like planets have been discovered so far.

• WEB LINKS •
http://kepler.nasa.gov

www.planethunters.org/

BECOME A SPACE TOURIST

There are lots of fun adventures to look out for. People are talking about trips into orbit or even sandboarding on Titan's hydrocarbon landscape!

• WEB LINKS •
www.newscientist.com/article/dn21400-astrophile-picture-yourself-on-a-sandboard-on-titan.html

www.spaceadventures.com

www.virgingalactic.com

TAKE PART IN THE SEARCH FOR EXTRATERRESTRIAL INTELLIGENCE (SETI)

Read up on the activities of the SETI Institute. You can search for alien life, too, by joining the SETI@home project. This is a scientific experiment that uses computers around the world to analyze radio telescope signals from space.

• WEB LINKS •
www.seti.org

http://setiathome.berkeley.edu

PREPARE YOURSELF FOR CLOSE ENCOUNTERS!

There's plenty of information out there to help you prepare yourself in the event of an alien invasion, should one ever take place! If you're in the mood for some reading, here's a useful Wikipedia page that describes many different types of visits from extraterrestrials.

• WEB LINK •
http://en.wikipedia.org/wiki/
Alien_invasion

DECODING A POSTCARD FROM SPACE

Remember this simplified version of Frank Drake's message puzzle from page 91? Did you manage to figure out what any of it meant? Below you can find out what the main parts of the message signify.

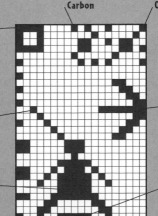

Carbon   Oxygen

The planetary system that the aliens live in: one star (top) and nine planets (below the star)

The symbols at the top show some of the most important life-building elements present on the alien world.

This line points to the planet that the aliens live on—the fourth from their sun.

The radio telescope that the aliens used to send the message

The basic body shape of the alien race

A short name that the aliens call themselves

GLOSSARY

As you read through this book, there are bound to be some words that are new to you. Here are some explanations of their meanings. Words in bold will lead you to other glossary entries.

adaptation
A feature or characteristic that allows an **organism** to live successfully in its environment. See also **evolution**.

air
Another name for our **atmosphere**, the layer of gases around our planet.

amino acid
One of a group of chemicals that make up **proteins**, which we get from food. Amino acids are the basic building blocks of your body's **cells**.

ammonia
A colorless gas made of **hydrogen** and **nitrogen** that dissolves in water.

anatomy
The body structure of an **organism**.

asteroid
A rocky, metallic object with no **atmosphere**. Asteroids orbit the Sun but are much smaller than planets.

astrobiology
The study of life in the universe.

atmosphere
A layer of gases that surrounds an object such as a **moon** or planet. The gases are held in place by **gravity**.

atmospheric pressure
The force exerted on a **moon** or a planet's surface by the weight of the atmospheric gases above that surface.

atom
An extremely tiny particle of matter. The basic unit of an **element**.

axis
The imaginary line around which an object (such as a planet) rotates.

bacterium (plural: **bacteria**)
A member of an extremely large group of single-celled microorganisms (tiny living things). See also **microbe**.

billion
One thousand million (1,000,000,000).

biochemistry
The chemistry of living **organisms**.

bioluminescence
Light created by living **organisms** through chemical reactions—for example, the light produced by glow-worms and fireflies.

byproduct
A **substance** that gets produced during the creation of another substance.

carbon
The chemical **element** that is the basis of all known life on Earth.

catalyst
A **substance** that increases the rate of a chemical reaction without being changed or used up by the reaction.

cell
The basic unit of living things: all known **organisms** are made up of one or more cells.

chemical compound
A **substance** formed from two or more **elements** that are combined through a chemical reaction.

climate
The general or average weather conditions of a place, as recorded over long periods of time.

cold-blooded
An animal is cold-blooded if its body temperature changes to match that of its natural surroundings.

comet
A small body made of rock and ice that travels around the Sun. Comets develop two "tails" (one of gas, one of dust) as they get closer to the Sun.

condense
To change from a gas into a liquid.

cosmos
A Greek word meaning "order," now used as another word for the universe.

crust
The uppermost layer of a rocky world.

density
The amount of matter (stuff) that is contained within a particular volume. (Volume is the space an object takes up.) The density of water, for example, is about 62 lb. per cu. ft. (1,000kg per m^3).

DNA (deoxyribonucleic acid)
A chemical that contains the genetic code used in the development and working of all known living things.

dwarf planet
A small world that **orbits** the Sun or another **star** with enough **gravity** to be spherical (ball shaped) or nearly so.

ecosystem
A living community of plants and animals sharing an environment with nonliving things such as **air**, soil, water, and sunlight.

element (metals and nonmetals)
A pure **substance** made from only one type of **atom**. An element cannot be made any simpler than it is already.

equator
The imaginary line, or ring, that runs around the middle of a spherical world such as Earth.

evaporate
To change from a liquid into a gas.

evolution
The process by which living things evolve (change) gradually over many generations to become suited to their immediate environment.

exoplanet
A planet outside our solar system.

extinction
The dying out of a **species**.

fat
One of a group of chemical compounds that dissolve in organic (**carbon**-based) **solvents** but not in water.

frost line
The distance from a **star** where it is cool enough for water, **ammonia,** and **methane** to be frozen solid.

galaxy
A vast collection of **stars**, planets, gas, and dust, all held together by **gravity**.

gene
A tiny string of chemicals that acts as an instruction manual for each life form. Genes determine the characteristics, or genetic makeup, of every living thing.

genus
A category used in biology to describe a group of closely related **species**.

gravity
The invisible force of attraction between objects in the universe created by the **mass** of those objects. For example, the **Moon orbits** Earth because Earth is more massive. But the Moon's gravity also has a pulling effect on Earth, causing the tides of the oceans.

habitable zone
Also known as a "Goldilocks" zone or life zone. The region around a **star** where liquid water can exist on the surface of a planet or **moon**.

habitat
The natural home or environment of a particular **species** of plant or animal.

helium
The second-lightest and second-most common **element** in the universe.

hydrogen
The lightest and most commonly occurring **element** in the universe.

hydrothermal vent
A crack in the ocean floor where water heated by volcanic activity (under the ocean floor) jets out.

intelligence
The ability to gain knowledge and skills and to use them in life.

intergalactic
Between two or more **galaxies**.

interplanetary
Between or among planets.

iron
A metal **element**. Iron is the most common element in Earth's outer and inner core (central region).

light-year
A unit of length, used in astronomy to measure vast distances. One light-year is just over 6 **trillion** miles (10 trillion km).

lipid
One of a large group of chemicals that includes **fats** and some vitamins.

main-sequence star
A **star,** such as our Sun, that is in the **hydrogen**-burning phase of its life.

mass
The amount of matter (stuff) that something contains. The mass of objects creates the effects of **gravity**.

matrix
An environment or material in which something develops or evolves.

metal
A shiny, pliable **element**. A good conductor of electricity and heat.

meteoroid
A sand- or boulder-sized piece of space debris. One that falls to Earth and survives impact is called a meteorite.

methane
A naturally occurring gas made up of the **elements hydrogen** and **carbon**.

microbe
A **bacterium,** or microscopic **organism**.

migrate
To move from one place to another.

Milky Way
The galaxy that contains our solar system (the Sun and orbiting objects).

million
One thousand thousand (1,000,000).

mineral
A nonliving **substance**, such as gold, formed by natural processes on Earth.

molecule
A group of two or more **atoms** held together extremely tightly.

molten
When something is liquefied (reduced to liquid form) by heat.

moon
A world that **orbits** a planet.

NASA
The National Aeronautics and Space Administration, based in the U.S.

nitrogen
The gas that now makes up about 78 percent of Earth's **atmosphere**.

nuclear fusion
The process in which light **atoms** fuse (join) together to make heavier ones, releasing energy as they do so.

nutrient
A **substance** that nourishes an **organism** so that it can live and grow.

orbit
The path of one object around another in space, created and maintained by the **gravity** of the objects.

organic compound
A **carbon**-based compound made up of **amino acid molecules**.

organic life
Living, **carbon**-based **organisms**.

organic matter
Matter (stuff) made up of **organic** (**carbon**-based) **compounds**.

organism
Any living thing that is able to grow and develop, reproduce, and respond to stimuli (happenings around it).

oxygen
The gas in our **atmosphere** that is used in **respiration** (breathing) to produce energy and enable the **cells** of living things to function.

parent star
A **star** that has a system of planets and other bodies orbiting around it.

particle
A tiny part of something. **Atoms** and **molecules** are often called particles.

photosynthesis
The process by which **organisms** convert carbon dioxide and water into food using sunlight. In this reaction, **oxygen** is released as a **byproduct**.

phylum (plural: phyla)
A group of animals that all have a similar anatomy (body plan).

protein
A **chemical compound** with a specific biological function: proteins are needed by the body for cell growth and repair.

radiation
Energy that travels through space, such as light and radio waves.

respiration
The process by which plants and animals release energy from food.

solvent
A liquid in which other **substances** can dissolve to create a "solution."

species
A particular type of animal or plant.

star
A huge ball of gas in space, usually glowing owing to the release of energy in the form of heat and light.

substance
A material with a definite chemical composition (makeup).

supernova
The explosion of a massive **star** (one that is at least eight times more massive than our Sun) or the sudden explosion of a "white dwarf" star in a binary (twin) star system.

trillion
One million million (1,000,000,000,000).

water cycle
The cycle of processes by which water moves between Earth's oceans, **atmosphere**, and land. It **evaporates** from rivers, lakes, and oceans and becomes water vapor in the air; it falls back to Earth's surface as precipitation (rain and snow, for example) and also freezes on parts of the surface as solid ice.

INDEX

HINTS AND TIPS FOR AN ALIEN HUNTER

Here are some more things you could do to help you think like a real-life, fully-fledged alien hunter . . .

• TIP ... ... at the
observ... ... ...nk
you ... ...they
pla... ...u will
...iety
...ons.

• TIP...
in th... ...n
ambit... ...on
are kn... ...any
arou... ...e've
hor...
liste...
he... ...ens.
...ter's
...hink
...of
• TIP... ...alien
sm... ...own.
Sor... ...from
appli... ...u in
you... ...d of
sor... ...be
a... ...en
...u

• T...
Look...
crys...
muse...
exam...
ino...
Ea...
ou...

...UCK
...ting!